THE REGIME OF THE STAY-LACE

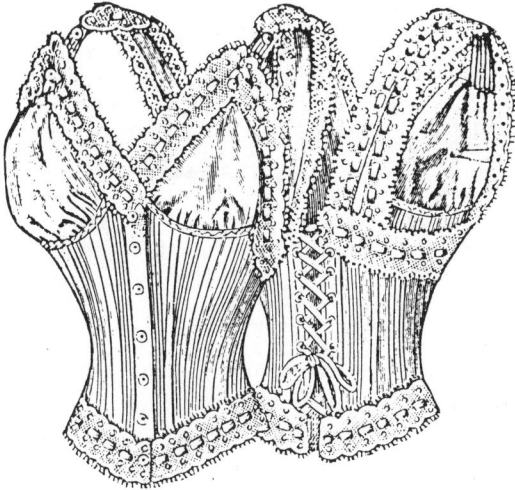

1

© 1995 Peter Farrer   **ISBN 0 9512385 3 1**
Published by Karn Publications Garston.
63 Salisbury Road, Garston, Liverpool L19 0PH.

Phototypeset and printed in England by Wilton Printing Company,
239B Preston Road, Wembley, Middlesex HA9 8PE.

THE REGIME OF THE STAY-LACE

A FURTHER SELECTION OF LETTERS FROM VICTORIAN NEWSPAPERS
Edited by PETER FARRER

KARN

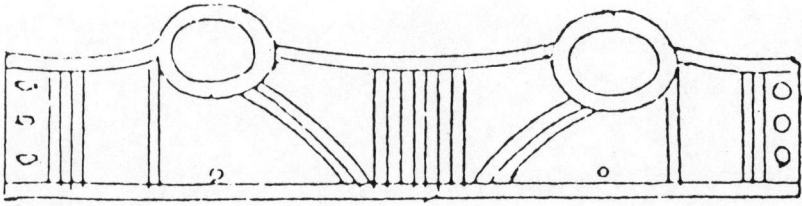

(a)

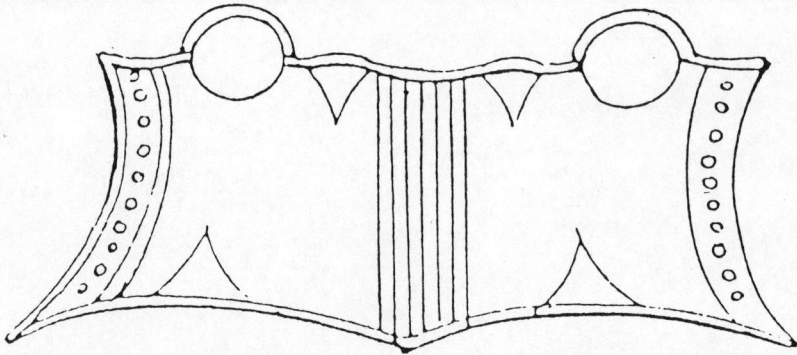

(b)

1.   (a) Child's Little Stay (fig. 33). (b) An Older Child's Stay (fig. 29),
The Workwoman's Guide (1838), Plate 11 (enlarged).

CONTENTS

LIST OF ILLUSTRATIONS
COLOUR AND PHOTOGRAPHIC PLATES

ILLUSTRATIONS IN THE TEXT   **Page**

ILLUSTRATIONS IN THE TEXT (contd.)

THE REGIME OF THE STAY-LACE

A FURTHER SELECTION OF LETTERS FROM VICTORIAN NEWSPAPERS

Edited by PETER FARRER

ACKNOWLEDGEMENTS

I wish to thank Anthea Jarvis, Keeper of The Gallery of English Costume, Platt Hall, Manchester, for obtaining the illustrations of Staybands and Mr David Yates Mason and the Norwich Record Office for information about the Paraman family.

Lord Curzon's notes on his 'School-Room Days' are reproduced by courtesy of the Trustees of the Kedleston Estate. The file may be seen at the Oriental India Office Collections of the British Library at Blackfriars Road, London.

The following libraries have been consulted: The British Library, The Newspaper Library, Colindale, The Bodleian, Cambridge University Library, The Victoria and Albert Museum, The Gallery of English Costume, Manchester Central Library, Liverpool City Libraries and the Libraries of the University of Liverpool and of Liverpool John Moores University.

I also thank Chris Wilson for invaluable help with production and my wife, Anne Brogden, for her continuing support and for help in finding and preparing the cover and illustrations.

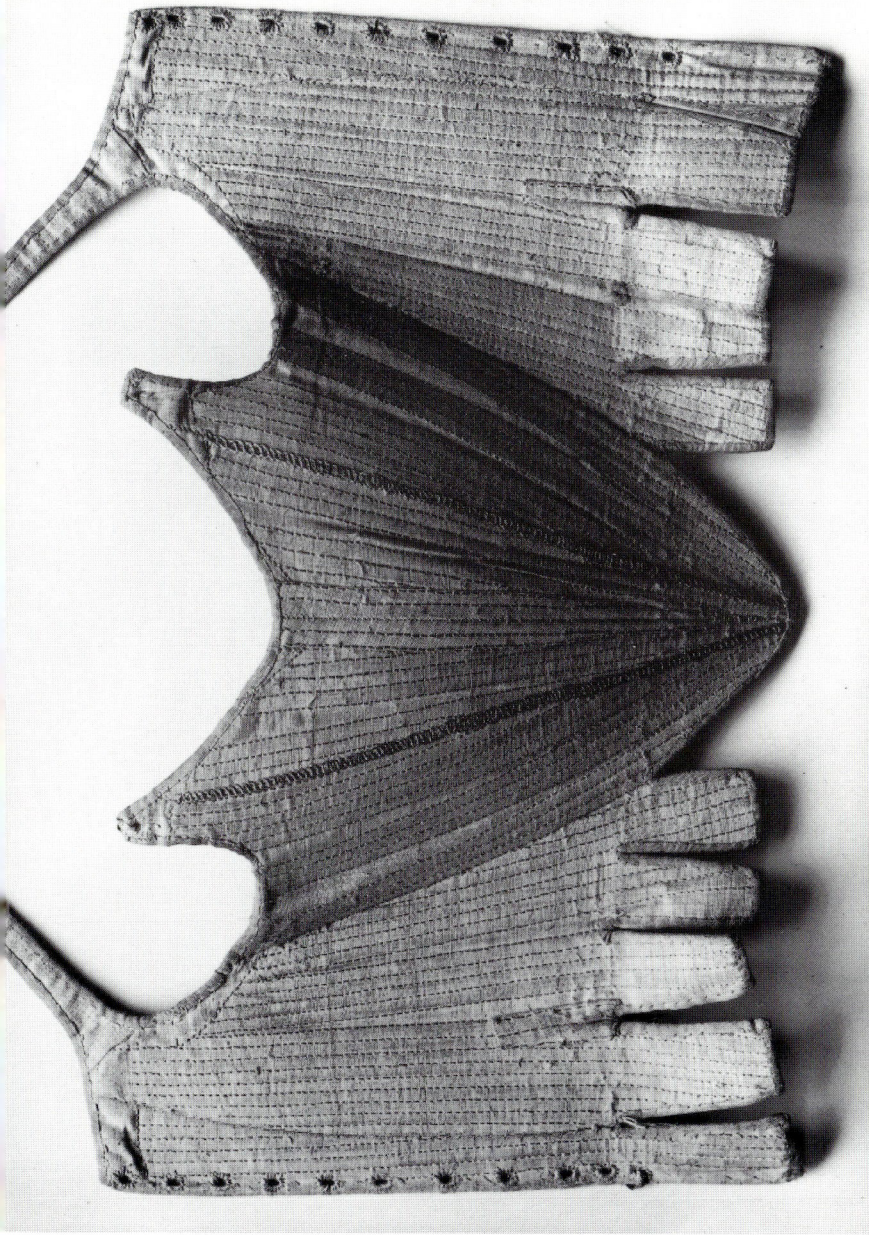

i. The stays worn by the effigy of Robert Sheffield, Marquess of Normanby, died 1715 aged three.
Courtesy the Dean and Chapter of Westminster.

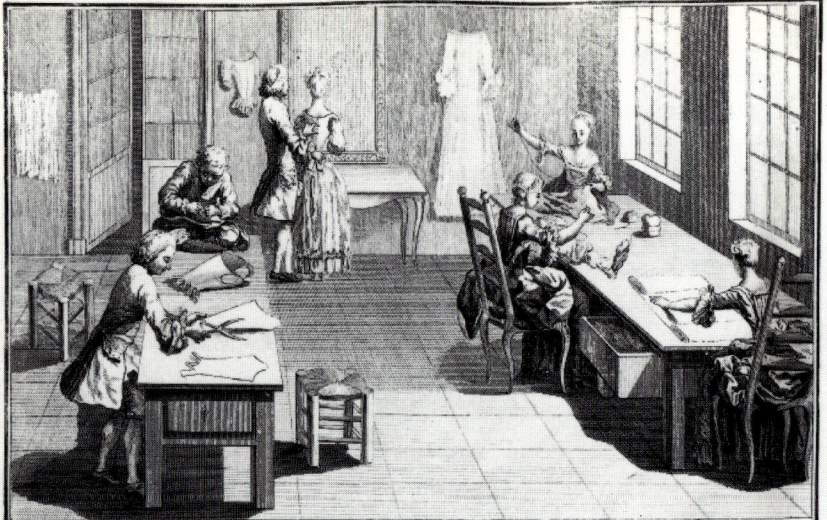

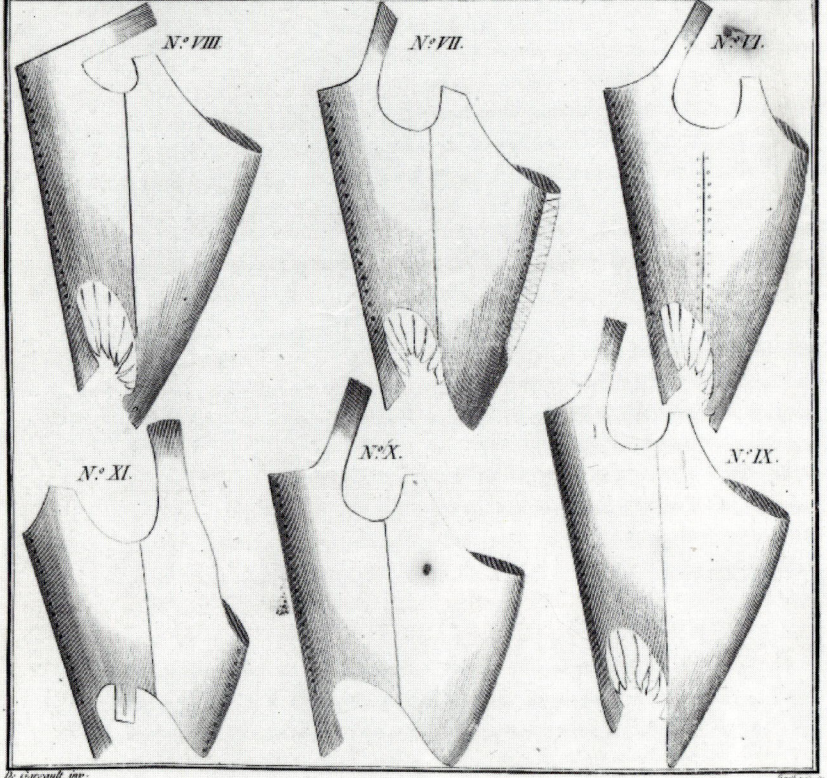

ii. Diagrams of stays: Francois A. de Garsault, L'Art du Tailleur (Paris: 1769).
   Plate XIII

THE REGIME OF THE STAY-LACE

A FURTHER SELECTION OF LETTERS FROM VICTORIAN NEWSPAPERS

Edited by PETER FARRER

PREFACE

My recent book *Borrowed Plumes* (1994) was a continuation of *Men in Petticoats* with letters from 1901 to 1912. The present work is an expansion or amplification of that book to include letters in the Victorian period on the wearing of stays by boys and the use of female clothing for disciplinary or punitive purposes. As before the letters are reproduced in chronological order by newspaper. In the first two chapters I shall give some general information about stays for children and about the usual clothing of small boys in the nineteenth century and try to describe the circumstances in which this punitive use came to be developed. In a final chapter I shall discuss other corroborative evidence.

Where available illustrations of stays have been provided. Otherwise the illustrations have been chosen on the one hand to show the normal costume of the small boy over the period, and on the other, to show the clothes of slightly older boys and girls so that the appearance of the boy when first breeched may be compared with that of girls of the same age, the greater the difference, the greater the embarrassment for the boy dressed as a girl.

Based on a drawing by Paul Kamm for the book *Der Gestiefelte Eros* (Booted Eros) by Hanns von Leydenegg (Berlin: 1932), which purports to be a true account of the early life of the author before the First World War. In the scene illustrated Hanns' aunt watches with satisfaction while Hanns is being fitted with corsets in the *Korsettsalon* of Mademoiselle Delaro of Berlin.

10

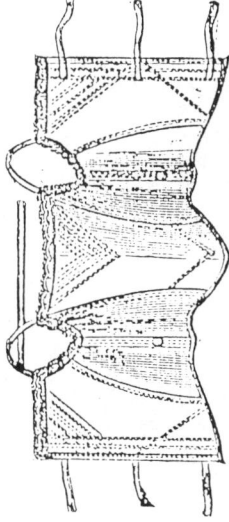
2. Madame Bayard's Improved Stays For Children.
Courtesy The Gallery of English Costume, Manchester.

11

No. 11.—CHEMISE FOR LITTLE GIRL.
No. 12.—SHIRT FOR LITTLE BOY.

3. (a) Chemise for Little Girl. (b) Shirt for Little Boy. (enlarged).

The Young Ladies' Journal, 1877, p. 313.

I

BOYS IN STAYS

Small boys, of course, wore stays as long as they retained the petticoats of childhood. In an article on the manufacture of stays published in *Once a Week* on 12 April 1862 (pp. 445-6) John Plummer estimated the number of women, children and infants in the U.K. wearing stays as 12,000,000. He went on to say, 'This number might be largely increased by the addition of all the male children under five years of age'. One of the clothed effigies still preserved in the Norman undercroft of Westminster Abbey is that of Robert Sheffield, Marquess of Normanby, who was born on 11 December 1711 and died on 1 February 1715, just over three years old. He wears a corset eleven inches in length made of canvas quilted with yellow silk and stiffened with cane. 'In front the point is very low; there are straps with ribbons over the shoulders and four tabs over the hips. The corset is laced in the centre of the back with a string of plaited coloured silk with metal tags.'[1] There is a reference to a boy's stays in an account book for 1722: 'Making Kitty's coats and a pair of stays for Harry 3.1.0'. Harry was about six or seven at the time.[2]

Later in the eighteenth century, in his *L'Art du Tailleur*, Garsault included a section on 'Le Tailleur de corps de femmes et enfants (tailor of stays for women and children)', and he gives a side-view of a number of different types of stays. IX is for a girl, X for a boy and XI for a boy *à sa première culotte* (in his first pair of breeches). It is interesting to compare them. The girl's are pointed at the front and have several tabs at the sides; the boy's is less deep in front and is rounded at the bottom with no tabs at the sides. The stays for the boy in breeches are markedly different. They lace up in front and the shoulder-piece is in front. There is a small tab with a button hole over the hip to enable it to be attached to the belt of the breeches.[3]

Garsault's engravings were reproduced with slight differences in Denis Didérot's *L'Encyclopédie*.[4] By way of explanation this comment was included in the Supplement: 'C'est assez la coutume en France et dans une partie de L'Europe de faire porter des corps aux enfans, aux garcons jusqu'à ce qu'on les mette en culotte; les filles et les femmes en portent presque toute leur vie (It is even the custom in France and in parts of Europe to make children wear stays, boys until they are breeched; girls and women wear them almost all their lives)'.[5] But when the compiler of the Supplement came to comment on the stays for a boy in breeches he added this remark: 'quoique communément les garcons cessent de porter un corps lorsqu'ils sont en culotte (although boys normally give up wearing stays after breeching)'.[6]

An illuminating comment on the wearing of stays by boys at this time is made by the German medical writer Samuel Thomas von Soemmering.

From 1760 to about 1770 it was the fashion in Berlin, and other parts of Germany, and also in Holland a few years ago, to apply corsets to children. This practice fell into disuse, in consequence of its being observed, that children who did not wear corsets grew up straight, while those who were treated with this extraordinary care, got by it a high shoulder, or a hunch. Many families might be named, in which parental fondness selected the handsomest of several boys to put in corsets, and the result was that these alone were hunched. The deformity was attributed at first to the improper mode of applying the corsets, till it was discovered that no child thus invested grew up straight, not to mention the risk of consumption and rupture which were likewise incurred by using them.[7]

It is typical that in quoting Soemmering, 'Madame de la Santé' and W.B. Lord, who copied her work, both omit the words indicating the unfavourable effects of corseting chil dren, while Luke Limner (Sir John Leighton), who attacked tight-lacing, gives the correct gist of his remarks.[8] Nevertheless correspondents to *The Family Doctor* in 1893 quote evidence that military cadets in Russia during the Napoleonic wars were subjected to tight-lacing in stays. Following an article on 'The History of the Corset' in *The Queen* in 1863,[9] 'Eliza K.' made this comment: 'I hear from a friend, who resided some time in Vienna, that it was the practice in many families for the boys to wear corsets, especially those designed for the army.'[10] The first letter in this collection is from a man who claimed that he was introduced to the corset at an Austrian school,[11] while similar experiences were related of schools in France,[12] in Austria again[13] and in Germany.[14]

To return to small boys. Like girls they wore some form of stay or stay-band as soon as they could walk. *The Workwoman's Guide* by A Lady of 1838 illustrated two stays for children and described them thus.

CHILD'S LITTLE STAY:

This is made of fine jean, doubled, of three nails depth, and of the width required by the child. Cord runners are made in front, and at the backs, and buttons are put on, before and behind, for the drawers and flannels to be attached to.

AN OLDER CHILD'S STAY:

This is formed of double jean, and may be lined between with Irish linen. If it is preferred, all the runners may have cotton drawn through them, so as to admit of no bones.[15]

The Gallery of English Costume, Platt Hall, Manchester has in its collection a child's stayband of the period 1860-80 (1963.53) made of red wool lined with white cotton. It has shoulder straps of white tape and white tapes at each side which cross over at the back and tie in front. The depth is four inches and the chest twenty. They also have an advertisement of about the same date for:

MADAME BAYARD'S IMPROVED STAYS FOR CHILDREN. Shaped and fitted to good models, with shoulder braces combined to prevent stooping, thereby rendering them good figures. These improved stays are made of Scarlet, pale blue and pompadour sateen, lined throughout, and machine stitched for support. Every mother should see these admirable stays and they would not allow their children to wear the uncomfortable straight band hitherto used.

Information about the wearing of stays by boys comes from *The Englishwoman's Domestic Magazine* and other papers. 'A Constant Subscriber' asked about clothes for a boy of four.

Can you tell me in your next number what style of dress is worn for little boys of four years old, where to get nice patterns, and have them made up, and any pretty way of dressing the hair? Are not the 'Highland costumes' more suitable for slight figures, and can you give me any information about their undergarments also? [Knickerbocker suits are worn by boys of three and four years. The Highland costumes are very pretty for stout or slim boys. A flannel shirt and stays are usually worn beneath these suits. Messrs. Macdougall, 42, Sackville-street, Piccadilly, supply them.][16]

This reply does not say what would be worn under the stays. Girls and women wore chemises under their stays and I feel sure that small boys would also have worn a thin undergarment like a chemise. There is valuable confirmation of this in *The Young Ladies' Journal* of 1877. An engraving is given of a 'Chemise for Little Girl' and, partly covering it, of a 'Shirt for Little Boy.'[17] The boy's 'shirt' is in fact very like the girl's chemise; there is a small slit at the side as in a shirt and the trimming is slightly different..As a sleeveless cotton undergarment it is in effect a chemise and is clearly intended to be worn under stays. It is called a shirt simply because it is for a boy, and I imagine that most mothers or nurses did not trouble to make any distinction between boys and girls in this respect and that boys in stays normally wore girls' chemises underneath. What such stays were like can be seen in The dress-making Supplement of *The Englishwoman's Domestic Magazine* for December 1879 which contains engravings of a 'Corset for Boys' (1157) and a 'Corset for Girls' (1167). The former is described as follows:

> Corset for boys of 6 to 8 years old. Corset of white twill and white elastic, stitched with silk, and bound with silk ferret. Shoulder-straps of white elastic. Eyelet holes to lace at the back.

and the latter:

> Corset for girls of 7 to 9 years old. Corset of white twill, elastic, and whalebone, laced up the back. The front is trimmed with vandyked strip of embroidered cambric. Shoulder-straps of white elastic.[18]

It will be seen from these descriptions and the illustrations that as compared with the girls', the boys' stays are cut away at the sides and are not strengthened with whalebone. 'Florence' in *The Sketch* recommended for boys as well as girls Reast's patent 'Invigorator' corsets with their 'ingenious arrangement of shoulder straps' which 'keep the chest well expanded, while forming a support for the back'.[19]

As to the age up to which stays were worn, Elizabeth Haldane, born in 1862, wrote, 'Both sexes wore stays, though boys discarded them about the age of seven'.[20] 'Maud Elizabeth' was advised to keep up the stockings of her boy of eight by tying them to the stays with tapes.[21] There is, however, evidence that older boys wore stays. 'M.C.', who said she was a staymaker, wrote: 'I can also inform "A Widower" that my son was fitted with stays when seven years old, and that he continues to wear them now that he is married'.[22] In a letter published in 1871, 'An Old Stay-Wearer' wrote: 'When a very weakly, delicate, growing lad, my mother, a strong-minded, sensible, masculine woman, put me into stiff stays, thinking thereby to improve my health. From that time, and, I have always thought, in consequence of the adoption of the stays, my health did greatly improve'.[23] In the unlikely pages of *The English Mechanic and World of Science and Art* a correspondent calling himself 'Corset' stated on 8 August 1873 that even as a child he had worn 'ordinary stay bodices.' He and two others, 'Evelyn H. Stanley'[24] and '72'[25] said that they were given ladies' stays to wear at the age of thirteen or fourteen for spinal disorders.

I have mentioned schools on the Continent. Several correspondents in *The Family Doctor* claimed that they had worn corsets for the purposes of drill or discipline at small English private schools.[26] 'John Sullivan' asserted that fifty years ago stays were the normal wear for the boys at 'a large boarding establishment for young gentlemen' at a University town near the sea. The wealthier boys at the parish school also wore stays.[27]

'Medicus Parens' argued that boys as well as girls should be subjected to 'corset discipline' for the benefit of their characters.[28] Several ladies wrote in to describe 'the regime of the staylace' which they had imposed on the unruly youths in their charge.[29] These letters are very similar in style with the same phrases recurring. A favourite device seems to have been the padlocked corset, which is also mentioned in the letters describing the tight-lacing of girls. The letter from 'White Cat' is particularly extreme. She has arranged with her corsetiere to have corsets made for her nephew. She then takes him into the shop and orders corsets for him in front of all the assistants, a customer and her two daughters. 'Tamed' related a similar incident in *Modern Society*.[30] The advocates of corsets for boys received both support and criticism from other readers. The three lady correspondents just mentioned were all severely rebuked. 'Trim Waist,' in particular, was violently attacked by a woman who gave her name and address as 'Elizabeth Henrietta Higgins of 35, Ackers Street, Manchester', a genuine address with 'Joseph Higgins' shown as occupier in the contemporary street directory. Similar responses were aroused by 'Amy Canning' in *Society* in 1899-1900.

In what I have discussed so far boys have worn stays for support as children, for their figures, deportment or health as youths and now as a form of penance or means of instiling moral improvement. Feminine footwear and gloves have also been employed in the last procedure. All along, however, in the same newspapers and magazines other correspondents have been describing or recommending something much more drastic, namely the wearing of complete female attire as a punitive or reforming measure. In the next chapter I shall say some-

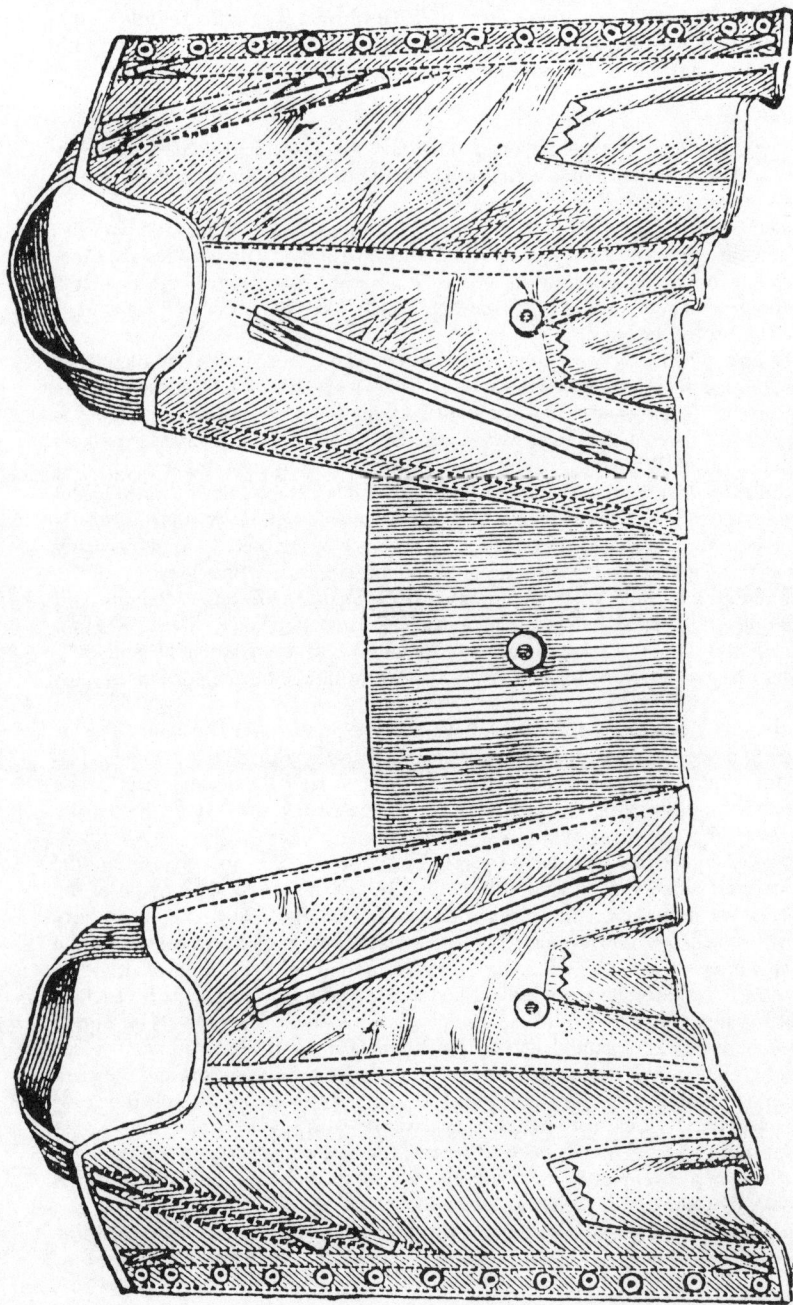

1,157.—BOY'S CORSET.

4. Boy's Corset. *The Englishwoman's Domestic Magazine,*
Supplement, December 1879, No. 1157.
By permission of the Syndics of Cambridge University Library.

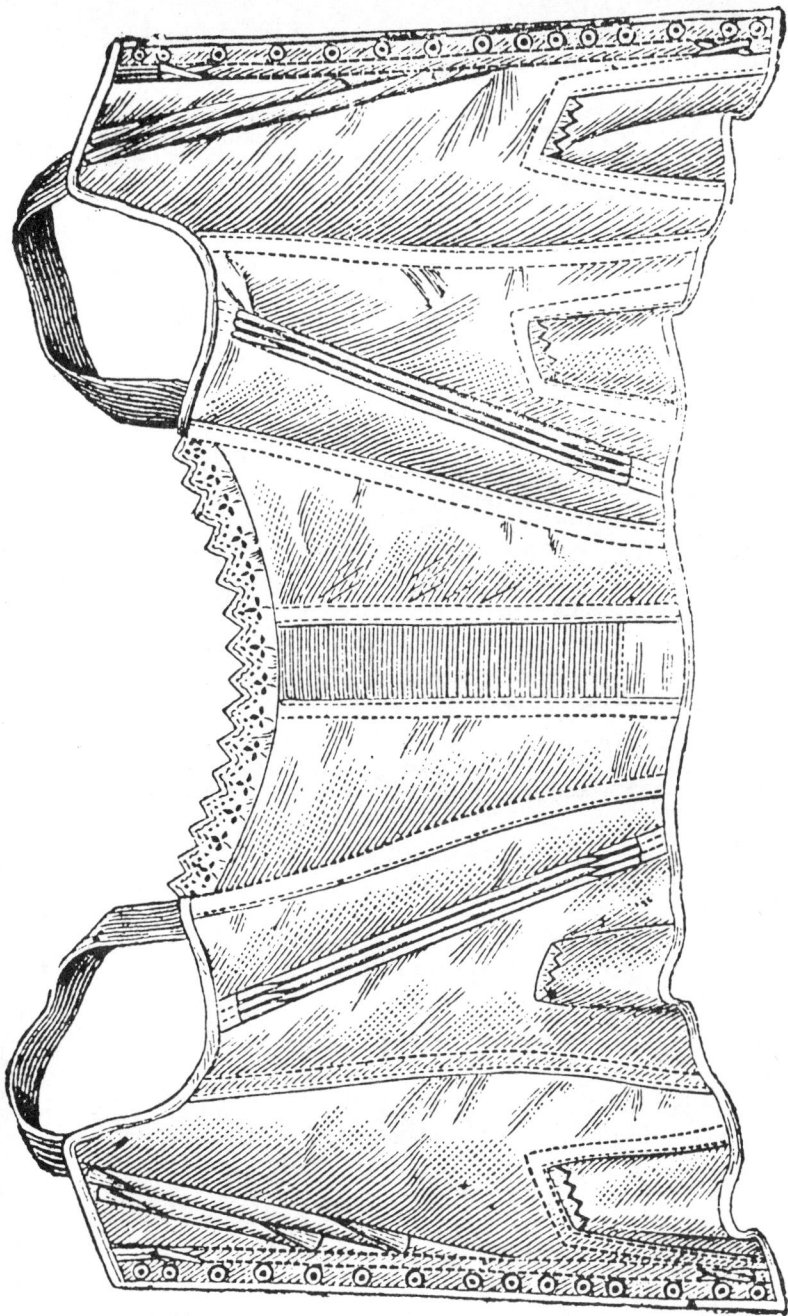

1,167.—GIRL'S CORSET.

5. Girl's Corset. *The Englishwoman's Domestic Magazine,*
Supplement, December 1879, No. 1167.
By permission of the Syndics of Cambridge University Library.

thing about boys' clothes in general and try to explain the social background in which the idea of the punishment came to be formulated and put into practice.

1   L.E. Tanner and J.L. Nevinson, 'On some late funeral effigies in Westminster Abbey', *Archaeologia*, 85 (1935), pp. 169-202. For a colour photograph of the fully clothed figure, see page 24 of the booklet on 'The Chapter House, The Pyx Chamber and Treasury, The Undercroft Museum' published by English Heritage.

2   The Furnese accounts, Guildford MSS., K.A.O., cited by Phillis Cunnington and Anne Buck, *Children's Costume in England 1300-1900* (London: Adam and Charles Black, 1965), reprinted 1972, p. 109.

3   Francois Alexandre de Garsault, *L'Art du Tailleur* (Paris, 1769), p. 45 and plate XIII. For a full extract from Garsault see F. Libron and H. Clouzot, *Le Corset dans L'Art et Les Moeurs du xiii au xx siècle (Paris, 1933), pp. 139-148, and for an English version, Norah Waugh, Corsets and Crinolines* (London: Batsford, 1954), pp. 153-5.

4   *Recueil de Planches* (Paris, 1771), VIII, Plate xxiii, 'Tailleur d'habits et tailleur de corps'.

5   Denis Didérot, *Supplément aux Dictionaires des Sciences, des Arts et des Métiers* (Paris, 1776), II, 615 (s.v. 'Corps ou Corps A Baleine').

6   Denis Didérot, *Supplément, etc.* (Paris, 1777), IV, 929 (s.v. 'Tailleur de Corps').

7   Samuel Thomas von Soemmering, *Ueber die Wirkungen der Schnuerbrueste* . . . (Berlin, 1793). I have, however, taken this translation from William Coulson, *On Deformities of the Chest* (London, 1836), pp. 53-4. He translates Soemmering's title as 'Effects of Compression of the waist by the Use of Corsets'.

8   Madame de la Santé, *The Corset Defended* (London: T.E. Carler, 1865) p. 8; W.B.L[ord], *The Corset and the Crinoline* (London: Ward, Lock, and Tyler, [1868]), p. 135; Luke Limner, *Madre Natura versus the Moloch of Fashion* (1870), fourth edition (London: Chatto & Windus, 1874), p. 60.

9   *The Queen*, 5 December 1863, p. 376.

10   *The Queen*, 19 December 1863, p. 411.

11   'Walter', *The Englishwoman's Domestic Magazine*, November 1867, p. 613.

12   *Modern Society*, 17 August 1889, p. 1018.

13   *The Family Doctor*, 13 May 1893, p. 172.

14   *M.S.*, 22 July 1899, p. 1169.

15   *The Workwoman's Guide by a Lady* (1838) second edition (London, 1840), facsimile edition (Doncaster: Bloomfield Books and Publications, 1975), p. 83 and Plate 11, figs. 33 and 29.

16   *E.D.M.*, April 1868, p. 223.

17   *The Young Ladies' Journal*, 14 (1877), 313.

18   The National Trust Collection of Costume at Killerton House has a pair of girl's cotton stays dated 1830 to 1850. There is a photograph and description in Clare Rose, *Children's Clothes since 1750* (London: Batsford, 1989), p. 76.

19   *The Sketch*, 26 April 1893, p. 789.

20   Elizabeth Haldane, *From One Century to Another* (London, 1937), p. 22, cited by Elizabeth Ewing, *History of Children's Costume* (London: Batsford, 1977), p. 101.

21   *E.D.M.*, June 1868, p. 326.

22   *E.D.M.*, August 1868, p. 112.

23   *Figure Training; or, Art The Handmaid of Nature*, by E.D.M. (London: Ward, Lock, and Tyler, [May 1871]), p. 51.

24   *The English Mechanic*, 24 March 1876.

25   op. cit., 14 April 1876.

26   *F.D.*, 'Eperon', 28 July 1888; 'Admirer of Pretty Feet', 8 June 1889 and 21 January 1890; 'R.D.B.', 29 June 1889 and 'Curb', 7 May 1892.

27   *F.D.*, 29 August 1891.

28   *F.D.*, 18 May 1889, 28 September 1889 and 17 September 1890.

29   *F.D.*, 'Finished Figure', 31 August 1889; 'Trim Waist', 14 December 1889, 28 December 1889 and 12 April 1890 and 'White Cat', 13 September 1890.

30   *M.S.*, 22 July 1899, p. 1169.

II

UNDER PETTICOAT GOVERNMENT

Until the early years of this century small boys were dressed in a similar way to girls, in dresses, tunics, Russian blouses, kilts and smocks, sometimes with the addition of pinafores or overalls. The age at which they were 'breeched' varied at different periods and among different classes.

Until the 1770's a boy of five or six exchanged a girl's frock for a smaller version of adult male costume. About that time a transitional costume was introduced, long trousers worn with a jacket or tunic, the most popular form of which was the combined top and trousers known as 'the skeleton suit.' It was not the dress of an adult male, but it was decidedly boyish and distinct from the dress of girls. It became the fashion for a boy to start wearing a skeleton suit as early as three or four. On the other hand when a doting mother held sway the age might be later. From the first paragraph of Disraeli's (1804-1881) first novel, *Vivian Grey*, published in 1826, it appears that the eponymous hero was not breeched until he was nearly ten:

We are not aware that the infancy of Vivian Grey was distinguished by any extraordinary incident. The solicitude of the most affectionate of mothers, and the care of the most attentive of nurses, did their best to injure an excellent constitution. But Vivian was an only child, and these exertions were therefore excusable. For the first five years of his life, with his curly locks and his fancy dress, he was the pride of his own and the envy of all neighbouring establishments; but, in process of time, the spirit of boyism began to develop itself, and Vivian not only would brush his hair straight and rebel against his nurse, but actually insisted upon being–breeched! At this crisis it was discovered that he had been spoiled, and it was determined that he should be sent to school. Mr. Grey observed, also, that the child was nearly ten years old, and did not know his alphabet, and Mrs. Grey remarked that he was getting ugly. The fate of Vivian was decided.

Nevertheless the fashion for the skeleton suit which lasted until about 1830 probably reduced the average age at which boys were breeched. The skeleton suit, however, was gradually replaced by another style of transitional costume which became more and more feminine. A boy of three might still leave off his child's frock, but he would go into a tunic with plain long trousers underneath. For the next thirty years the tunic got longer and fuller, more like a frock, while the trousers became shorter, but still visible, and more ornamental. To a modern eye a boy of five or six of the 1850's looks like a girl in a wide-skirted frock worn over lace trimmed drawers. It is clear from French fashion magazines that Parisian boys wore crinolines under their dresses. A boy's frock would, of course, be of a slightly different cut from a girl's, and not made in the most feminine of materials and colours. For a party frock a boy could wear plaid satin or blue velvet, but not pink shot silk. Even under the supposedly male kilt a boy might wear a lace trimmed petticoat and drawers and look very girlish. Later in the century, when the sailor suit came in, the small boy wore the girls' version, with a skirt.

In 1860 the introduction of the knickerbocker suit brought earlier emancipation to some small boys, but the Russian blouse, tied at the waist, with a longish skirt, continued to give a skirted look to boys of nine or ten. For evening too, knickerbockers were made of velvet and led to the Fauntleroy costume, which, while entirely suitable and fashionable for the seven year old Fauntleroy, was resented by older boys. Smocks, pinafores and overalls were also frequently worn by boys. Long hair, often elaborately waved or curled, usually accompanied the petticoat stage and sometimes beyond.

To sum up, it is as if in the nineteenth century a war was fought between the male and the female principle over how the small boy should be dressed. At one period with one type of garment the male principle was in the ascendant, at other times and with other garments the female. The male principle prevailed with the skeleton suit, the kilt, knickerbockers and sailor suits, the female fought back with lace-trimmed underwear, velvet and satin, and with smocks and pinafores. Certainly throughout the nineteenth century, small boys, while under feminine care, under petticoat government as it were, wore petticoats themselves. It was usual to refer to a boy of this age as being 'in petticoats.' The earliest example of this use of the phrase cited by *The Oxford English Dictionary* is from Captain Marryat's novel of 1837, *The Dog Fiend; or, Snarleyyow*. The author is speaking of the evil Lieutenant Vanslyperken, master of the naval cutter, the *Yungfrau*, and his mother. 'The old woman did not appear to be fond of him, although she treated him as child, and executed her authority as if he were still in petticoats' (chapter 14). A later example occurs in *Robert Elsmere* by Mrs Humphrey Ward published in 1888. When Elsmere and his wife visit the squire, the squire's wife says, 'Roger, here are Mr. and Mrs. Robert Elsmere. Mr. Elsmere, the squire remembers you in petticoats, and I'm not sure that I don't too.'[1]

Against this background of female supremacy over the early years of boyhood, women sought to extend the period of their rule in two ways. On the one hand some mothers or female guardians, where they had the power or opportunity, kept their boys in a petticoated state for longer than usual. I have already mentioned the fictional case of Vivian Grey. Elizabeth Barrett Browning was a mother who did this in real life to her only son, Robert Wiedeman Barrett Browning, 'Penini'. Another extension of petticoat rule was achieved by repetticoating boys who had already been breeched as a method of punishment. Much has been written about the corporal punishment inflicted on English children in the nineteenth century and the correspondence about it to be found in the British press. What has been wholly ignored or overlooked is this entirely different form of punishment whereby a boy is required to wear an article of girl's clothing or complete girl's attire, for long or short periods, in order to produce shame and humiliation.

Most boys are brought up to, or have ingrained in them, an underlying aversion towards anything girlish in their attire or activities. Wearing or doing anything of a girlish nature thus causes shame and embarrassment. An interesting expression of this feeling comes in Mrs Sherwood's famous and amazingly popular *The History of the Fairchild Family; or, the Child's manual: being a collection of stories calculated to shew the importance and effects of a religious education*.[2] The first part of this work was published in 1818, but the second and third parts not until 1842 and 1847 respectively. Although the narrative is continuous through the three parts, no attempt is made to keep to the period in which the first part was written. In parts II and III Queen Victoria is on the throne and the frontispieces reflect the fashions of the eighteen-forties. There are very few references to dress in the first two parts, and none at all to boys' dress in Part I. In the first chapter of Part II, Henry is described as paying a visit 'in his Sunday dress', but no details are given. In chapter 7 a typical incident of childhood is described in these terms:

A great sturdy boy in petticoats, of about four years old, followed little Miss Jane, roaring and blubbering because Jane had pinched him in return for the scratch.

This is another early use of the phrase 'in petticoats'. I suggest that by this date (1842) when boys remained in petticoats for a longer period than in the days of the skeleton suit, it became more worthy of note. Mrs. Sherwood, born in 1775, would have seen it as change of fashion. No doubt Mrs Sherwood also had a moral purpose in relating the incident: the pinch is retribution for the scratch. Thus the 'sturdy' boy gets the worst of it in his skirmish with the 'little' girl, and already dressed like a girl, is reducd to tears.

Clothes, especially boys' clothes, are of much greater importance in Part III published in 1847. In the first few chapters we are mainly concerned with Henry Fairchild and the clothes he wears, why he wears them and what happens to them (he falls in the pig-swill). For this part Mrs Sherwood received the help of her daughter, Mrs Sophia Streeten, afterwards Mrs Kelly.

Perhaps this emphasis on clothes is attributable to Mrs Streeten's influence. In chapter 1 the family are setting out for their new home, The Grove, near Reading. Henry is to go with the servants Betty and John in the old carriage. In case it might be cold, Betty says that she will get Henry a shawl or cloak, but Henry objects:

> 'No, Betty!' exclaimed Henry, holding her back as she was about to dismount from the carriage; 'No, I won't have a shawl or a cloak, that is like a girl. I hate to be like a girl, or dressed like a girl. I won't have a shawl, Betty.'
>
> 'Master Henry,' said John, 'if you are to begin in this way, why I shall ask your papa to leave you behind; for how are we to get on if we are wrong in the first starting?'
>
> 'But John,' asked Henry, 'should you like to wear a shawl, or a cloak, like a woman; now should you , John?'
>
> 'Why, young master,' replied John, 'I can't say as how I should on broad daylight, and yet if I found it convenient to put on a woman's shawl or cloak or bonnet either, I have heard of many a wiser man than myself that would do it, and do it thankfully. The older you are, the less you would mind it, Master Henry.'[30]

Hearing all this, Henry's sister Emily persuades papa to lend Henry his large cloak. Henry was probably thinking of the childish frocks he wore up to the age of four or five. Henry is now nearly eight.

In the last century, but not before, women in charge of boys started to punish them by exploiting this natural aversion: they dressed them as girls. Sometimes this was done before and sometimes after corporal punishment, sometimes physical punishment was dispensed with altogether, the idea being that the embarrassment of being dressed as a girl in front of witnesses, especially female witnesses, constituted the punishment. It was a 'shaming technique' similar to making David Copperfield (1849-50) wear a placard on his back reading, 'Take care of him. He bites', or Hester Prynne in Hawthorne's *The Scarlet Letter* (also 1850) sew a scarlet 'A' on her breast. As such it was perhaps seen as a more humane or less brutal punishment than a beating, and perhaps reflects the reforms in educational methods advocated by people like Joseph Lancaster (1778-1838) and Andrew Bell (1753-1832). Placards recording offences and public confessions were also used as shaming techniques at the Quaker schools founded during the first half of the nineteenth century. No one of course advocated dressing boys as girls and many would think it at least as cruel as a flogging. Curiously no one seems to have thought of dressing a boy as a girl for punitive reasons until the nineteenth century. Presumably the rod was thought to be essential and the cross-dressing involved forbidden by the bible and not yet sanctioned by custom.

One of my purposes in compiling this collection is to establish that this punishment was actually carried out and to reprint all the printed material about it that I have been able to find up to 1900. I have already said that nobody advocated it. What is particularly striking is that nobody knows anything about it now. There is no mention of it in books about children's clothes and upbringing nor in histories of education, or even of punishment. No one seems to know anything about it, except readers of certain obscure reports of psychologists and connoisseurs of erotica. It is not known to students or biographers of the life of the Victorian boy. The purpose of this work is to provide that knowledge.

In its earliest manifestation the punishment arose as a way of letting the punishment fit the crime. Early hints of this are seen in two of the children's books in the Osborne Collection of the Toronto Public Library from which Leonard de Vries prepared his anthology, *Flowers of Delight*.[3] Elizabeth Turner's *The Daisy; or, Cautionary stories, in verse. Adapted to the ideas of children, from four to eight years old* was first published in 1807 and went into twenty-one editions by 1840. The following verses therefore conveyed their warning to children for over twenty years.

21

DRESSED OR UNDRESSED

When children are naughty, and will not be dressed,
    Pray, what do you think is the way?
Why, often I really believe it is best
    To keep them in night-clothes all day!

But then they can have no good breakfast to eat,
    Nor walk with their mother or aunt;
At dinner They'll have neither pudding nor meat,
    Nor anything else that they want.

Then who would be naughty, and sit all the day
    In night-clothes unfit to be seen?
And pray, who would lose all their pudding and play,
    For not being dressed neat and clean?[4]

Here the punishment envisaged could be applied to a lazy child of either sex. The punishment is to be made to wear inappropriate clothes, to wear night attire all day. The second item from the Osborne Collection is even more relevant. *Dame Truelove's Tales, now first published as useful lessons for little misses and masters* came out in 1817. In the story entitled 'Charles,' a boy complains about his girlish frock, but since he is still behaving like a child he has to remain dressed as one. Again the punishment fits the crime.

CHARLES

Charles was a fine boy of four years of age; his cheeks were like two red apples, for he spent a great part of the day in the garden, running about and rolling in the grass; that is, from seven o'clock in the morning till twelve, at which time his Grandpapa was ready to receive him and not sooner. The moment the clock struck that hour, away he ran and bounced into the room where he knew he was always welcome; and the old gentleman calling him to sit upon his knee, usually asked what he had been doing, and whether he had learnt his lesson. Charles was not very fond of his book, and his Grandpapa often told him that if he did not learn to read, when he grew up, he would be called Sir Charles DUNCE, and all the boys in the town would laugh at him; but he did not mind it much, he only kissed his Grandpapa, and said he would learn his lesson when he could find time. One day he entered the room, saying he was very unhappy indeed, and taking his seat upon his Grandpapa's knee, told him that little Johnny Gibson had got a jacket and trowsers, whilst he was kept like a girl in petticoats; and that he thought it was very hard upon him, 'a great boy as I am,' said he, 'more than four years old; there is my sister Maria always calling me Miss Charley, a little thing like her, no bigger than my thumb!'

'Indeed Charles, it is a very sad thing,' said his Grandpapa, 'but I must tell you that it is your own fault; John Gibson can read little Tales, and Dialogues in words of one syllable, and has had his jacket and trowsers as a reward for his attention to his learning, whilst you are so idle that you scarcely know your letters, you must therefore content yourself with your petticoats for some time longer.'

Charles was much ashamed and hung down his head for some minutes, but from that time he learnt his lesson every day, and never went to run in the garden till he had done it, so that in a few months he had the pleasure of seeing himself dressed in a jacket and trowsers, and equal in all respects to John Gibson, and every other boy of his age.[5]

In this story the traditional breeching of a boy is presented not as a stage in the process of growing up but as a reward for good behaviour and diligent application to lessons. Trousers are a prize while the continuation of petticoats is a penalty for idleness. This is an entirely new idea.

Something similar is suggested at the beginning of Part III of *The History of the Fairchild*

Family. We have seen that Henry hates anything girlish. His actual costume is described as follows:

> On the low seat between them was Henry, still wearing his petticoated jacket, for he was not eight years old, with a black girdle round his waist. Henry was to have a cloth jacket like a boy's jacket, made for him as soon as he reached the Grove; for his mamma thought he was old enough now for the change, but she wished him to look as young as he really was when he first made his appearance at their new home, for she knew the servants and people about would wish to flatter him and make a bustle about him as the future owner of the Grove; and he knew, that being but a little boy, he would be sure to do something silly if they flattered him much, and therefore the younger he looked the more excuse there would be for him (Part III, p. 8).

It is unlikely that a boy of seven would think about his clothes in the way described and accept the continuation of a childish mode of dress for the reasons ascribed to him. The description does, however, well illustrate the style of costume for boys at the time of writing. Henry is still wearing a transitional costume, a half-way stage between the girlish frock of early childhood and the breeches and jacket of assured boyhood. The 'petticoated jacket' was a sort of longish tunic buttoning at the front like a jacket, but still with an enveloping skirt round the legs. Underneath he wore long white trousers. Next day at the Grove he is fastened into a pinafore. What is interesting for our purposes is the attitude of the mother. She is deliberately keeping Henry in a childish costume for a moral purpose, in the hope of ensuring good behaviour or of mitigating the effects of bad behaviour. Her precautions are in vain. When they stop for refreshments at the Fairchild Arms, Mr. and Mrs. Bunce do flatter him and he does behave in a silly manner. John admonishes him:

> 'You ought to like them, Master Henry,' replied John, 'for they meant to be very kind to you; but yet I fancy you would not thank them if you had sense enough to know what a pretty figure you cut from their flattery. There were you lolling back in your chair with a piece of cake in your hand, at one moment, and the next busy with the spoon at the sugar-basin, searching out for the very largest lumps. Then you splashed yourself, too, with the beef-gravy, when you would help yourself a second time, when you knew as well as I did that you had had enough, and it was only for the pleasure of using a knife and fork in the dish that made you take it at all. Oh, Master Henry, Master Henry,' added John laughing, 'good Mrs. Bunce makes a very baby of you, and if you were to stay in her house awhile you would never be fit to be put into jackets and trowsers: you must keep to your pinafores and frocks, for the others would in a day not be fit to be seen.'

> 'I am sure, John,' said Henry, very angry, 'I am sure, John, that you know nothing about it. Mrs. Bunce is a very good woman, and she could not make a baby of me. I am too old to be made a baby of by her or anyone else' (Part III, pp. 20-21).

As in the story of 'Charles', we have the idea that the garments of childhood must be retained because the boy is still behaving in a childish way. Emancipation into boyish clothes depends not just on age and size, but on appropriate behaviour. Henry is only teased by John with the prospect of such a continuation of pinafores and frocks, while Charles is a younger boy still wearing a frock. These may be fictional examples, but they indicate that the idea of such punishments was present in the minds of these writers and their readers. I suggest that such passages in these much read books of Turner, Sherwood, Dickens and Hawthorne had the effect of familiarising people with the idea of imposing shameful clothing as a punishment. The final stage is for a boy who has graduated to normal boys' clothes to be dressed wholly as a girl.

This is where the correspondence in newspapers and magazines comes in. The first incident of this sort that I have been able to discover was reported by a contributor to the Supplement to *The Englishwoman's Domestic Magazine* for April 1870. This Supplement, which ran from April to December 1870, was devoted to letters about corporal punishment which had become too many for the normal correspondence column, 'The Englishwoman's Conversazione'. Not everyone, of course, agreed with corporal punishment and one of its opponents, 'Etonensis', suggested in its place love and shame, love being inspired by the kindness of his tutor at Eton and shame experienced at the hands of his governess. At least twenty years previously, the writer had been dressed in his sister's clothes by his governess for failing to learn his geography lesson. He had to stay in these clothes until he had learnt the lesson, joining his sisters for dinner so dressed. Thereafter the mere threat of the punishment was sufficient to make him behave. This is the first description of such an incident that I have been able to find. I have not found the slightest trace of such a punishment having been carried out on boys before then. Short of that, however, was the penitential costume imposed on the children of the Curzon family by their nurse, Miss Paraman, in the second half of the sixties. To the dunce's cap and placards announcing the crime she added a long petticoat for boys and girls alike. I go fully into this in the next chapter.

When the letter from 'Etonensis' was reprinted without acknowledgement in *Town Talk* in 1885 several further incidents were reported. At the age of fourteen John E.C.H. of Chicago, was actually put into the Kindergarten class of a school in Louisiana, dressed as a child of three or four, i.e. as a little girl. As will be shown there is a parallel in the treatment of slaves in the South during the same period. The punishment was also described in letters published in *Society* from 1899 to 1900, in *Modern Society* from 1909 to 1911 and in *Photo Bits* from 1910 to 1912. The letters in the two latter papers have been reproduced in my *Borrowed Plumes*.

1   Mary Augusta Ward (Mrs) (1851-1920), *Robert Elsmere*, (1888), Nelson's Library, (London: Thomas Nelson and Sons, [1907]), p. 223 (chapter 17).
2   Mary Martha Butt, afterwards Sherwood (1775-1851), *The History of the Fairchild Family; or, the Child's manual* (London: J. Hatchard, 1818-47). See also the article on Mrs Sherwood in DNB.
3   Leonard de Vries, *Flowers of Delight* (London: Dennis Dobson, 1965).
4   de Vries, pp. 45 and 227.
5   de Vries, pp. 86 and 227.

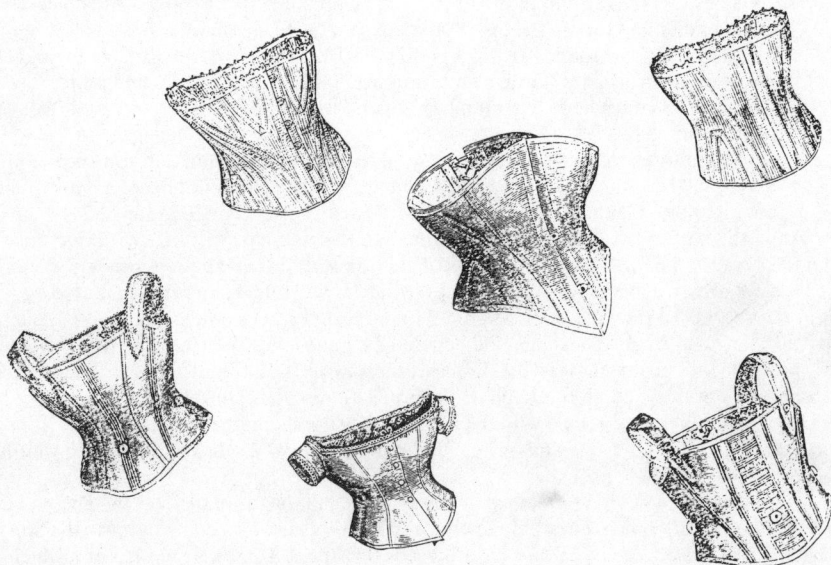

iii. Child's Stayband 1860-80: (a) Front. (b) Back. © *Manchester City Art Galleries.*

Fashions for August 1840.

iv. Fashions for August 1840.

Probably *The New Monthly Bell Assemblée*

III

THE ENGLISHWOMAN'S DOMESTIC MAGAZINE

The Englishwoman's Domestic Magazine was founded by Samuel Orchart Beeton in May 1852 when he was only twenty one. It was the first cheap monthly magazine for women of the middle classes, at a price of two pence instead of the usual shilling. From the start Beeton encouraged and made use of correspondence from readers. In the first issue there was a feature entitled 'Cupid's Letter Bag' in which Beeton undertook to advise correspondents on the subject of courtship. In the second series of the magazine, beginning in May 1860 and printed in a slightly larger size, Beeton introduced his 'Englishwoman's Conversazione,' adding a separate section for 'Answers to Correspondents' in May 1861.

Meanwhile Beeton had married Isabella Mayson on 10 July 1856, and she joined him in his journalistic ventures, contributing notes on household management and cookery, and compiling her classic *Book of Household Management*, a work which owed much to recipes supplied by readers, which appeared in twenty-four monthly parts from November 1859 to October 1861. A new series of the Magazine, again in a larger size, with a third set of volume numbers, began in January 1865, but in the next two years Beeton suffered two personal disasters. Mrs. Beeton died at the age of twenty-eight on 6 February 1865 after the birth of her fourth child, while the failure of Overend, Gurney & Co. on 5 May 1866 threatened him with financial ruin. Beeton came to an arrangement with Ward, Lock & Tyler, whereby they took over as publishers and he remained as editor of his existing magazines.

Under the new management, the magazine was redesigned. Plans for this were announced in November 1866 and put into effect from January 1867, in effect creating a fourth series, although the volumes were not renumbered. The new magazine included an enlarged 'Conversazione', as announced in December 1866: 'and at our Conversazione, the circle and extent of which we shall considerably enlarge, we expect a very great number of interesting subjects and interested people'. *The Englishwoman's Domestic Magazine* is notorious for the fact that the interesting subjects included corporal punishment and tight-lacing, although these had previously been treated in *The Family Herald and The Queen*. The subject of tight-lacing had been mentioned twice before in the Conversazione, in July 1862 when SERAPHINE wrote to ask, 'what is the smallest size waist known?' and in November 1863 when it was reported that A VICTIM had sent the editor 'eight closely-written pages–on a subject of very serious importance, that of having her poor ribs tortured into a fashionable figure'. There was also an article on 'The Human Form Divine' in September 1866.

In the new Conversazione the subject was introduced in the issue for March 1867, by 'A lady, dating from Edinburgh,' who complained about 'the most merciless system of tight-lacing' to which her daughter had been subjected 'at a large and fashionable boarding school near London.' The first reply was from STAYLACE, in April, who thought the letter was 'made up for a purpose'. To her 'the sensation of being tightly laced in a pair of elegant, well-made, tightly fitting corsets' was 'superb'. Numerous letters followed in the next few years, during which the arguments both for and against the corset and its uses were fully explored.

In November 1867 a man entered the debate. 'Walter' described how he had been forced to wear stays at an Austrian school. He was made to wear stays against his will, not as a punishment, but to smarten his figure and improve his deportment. The stays were part of his usual attire and he grew to like them. I am reproducing this letter in full together with one or two replies partly because of the element of compulsion, which is first seen in this letter and partly because his experience is echoed by other former schoolboys later in this collection.

THE CORSET QUESTION   NOVEMBER 1867 (p. 613).

Madam, May I be permitted for once to ask admission to your Conversazione, and to plead as excuse for my intrusion that I am really anxious to endorse your fair correspondent's, BELLE's, assertion that it is those who know nothing practically of the corset who are most vociferous in condemning it? Strong-minded women who have never worn a pair of stays, and gentlemen blinded by hastily-formed prejudice, alike anathematise an article of dress of the good qualities of which they are utterly ignorant, and which, consequently, they cannot appreciate. On a subject of so much importance as regards comfort (to say nothing of the question of elegance, scarcely less important on a point of feminine costume) no amount of theory will ever weigh very heavily when opposed by practical experience. 'The proof of the pudding' is a proverb too true not to be acted on in such a case. To put the matter to the actual test, can any of the opponents of the corset honestly state that they have given up stays after having fairly tried them, except in compliance with the persuasions or commands of friends, or medical advisers who seek in the much-abused corset a convenient first cause for an ailment that baffles their skill? THE YOUNG LADY HERSELF does not complain of either illness or pain, even after the first few months, while, on the other hand, STAYLACE, NORA, and BELLE bring ample testimony, both of themselves and their schoolfellows, as to the comfort and pleasure of tight-lacing. To carry out my first statement as to the truth of BELLE's remark, those of the opposite sex who, either from choice or necessity, have adopted this article of attire, are unanimous in its praise, while even among an assemblage of opponents a young lady's elegant figure is universally admired while the cause of it is denounced.

From personal experience, I beg to express a decided and unqualified approval of corsets. I was early sent to school in Austria, where lacing is not considered ridiculous in a gentleman as it is in England, and I objected in a thoroughly English way when the doctor's wife required me to be laced. I was not allowed any choice, however. A sturdy *mädchen* was stoically deaf to my remonstrances, and speedily laced me up tightly in a fashionable Viennese corset. I presume my impressions were not very different from those of your lady correspondents. I felt ill at ease and awkward, and the daily lacing tighter and tighter produced inconvenience and absolute pain. In a few months, however, I was as anxious as any of my ten or twelve companions to have my corsets laced as tightly as a pair of strong arms could draw them. It is from no feeling of vanity that I have ever since continued to wear them, for, not caring to incur ridicule, I take good care that my dress shall not betray me; but I am practically convinced of the comfort and pleasantness of tight-lacing, and thoroughly agree with STAYLACE that "the sensation of being tightly laced in an elegant, well-made, tightly-fitting pair of corsets is superb." There is no other word for it. I have dared to make this avowal because I am thoroughly ashamed of the idle nonsense that is constantly being uttered on this subject in England. The terrors of hysteria, neuralgia, and, above all, consumption, are fearlessly promised to our fair sisters if they dare to disregard preconceived opinions, while, on the other hand, some medical men are beginning slowly to admit that they cannot conscientiously support the extravagant assertions of former days. 'Stay torture,' 'whalebone vices,' and 'corset screws,' are very terrible and horrifying things upon paper, but when translated into *coutil* or satin they wear a very different appearance in the eyes of those most competent to form an opinion. That much perfectly unnecessary discomfort and inconvenience is incurred by the purchasers of ready-made corsets is doubtless true; the waist measure being right, the chest–where undue constriction will naturally produce evil effects–is very generally left to chance. If then the wearer suffers, who is to blame but herself? The remarks, echoed by nearly all your correspondents, that ladies have the remedy in their own hands by having their stays made to measure is too self-evident for me to wish to enlarge upon it; but I do wish to assert and insist that if a corset allows sufficient room in the chest, the waist may be laced as tightly as the wearer desires without fear of evil consequences; and, further, that the ladies themselves who have given tight-lacing a fair trial, and myself and schoolfellows, converted against our will, are the only jury entitled to pronounce authoritatively on the subject, and that the comfortable support and enjoyment afforded by a well-laced corset quite overbalances the theoretical evils that are so confidently prophesied by outsiders.   WALTER.

This letter provoked two requests for information from Walter, and a reply from him.

SCHOOLS IN AUSTRIA   JANUARY 1868 (p. 54).
A LADY, who is about to send her son (twelve years of age) to a school in Vienna, would be much obliged to our correspondent WALTER if he will inform her whether the active boyish games, so much rejoiced in by English schoolboys, are discouraged in Austria? or what are the amusements indulged in by the young gentlemen of the Viennese schools?

AUSTRIAN SCHOOLS   FEBRUARY 1868 (p. 110).
Can your correspondent WALTER (who says he was educated in Austria) tell me where prospectuses of Austrian schools can be obtained, or give me any information thereon? If he would give an address where I could write to him under his nom-de-plume I should be still further obliged to him, as I am thinking of sending two of my sons to be educated abroad, and am most anxious to learn all I can of foreign schools. I have heard that education is cheaper and better in Austria than in Germany.

                                                         PATER.

SCHOOLS IN AUSTRIA   MARCH 1868 (p. 166).
WALTER L.S. writes:
In reply to A LADY I beg to state that active boyish games are not discouraged in Austria, although those in vogue there (at least in my time) bear little resemblance to those most in favour among English schoolboys. The great outdoor game was played with a large ball about twelve inches in diameter. This was whirled round by means of a short cord, serving as a handle, and by this means propelled towards the goal. In reality it was not unlike football played with the hands and arms instead of the hands and feet, and was deservedly popular. We also had a game somewhat similar to 'prison base.' Cricket, I believe, is now played, but while I was in Austria it was a delicate exotic. Gymnastics and fencing were daily occupations, and about twice a week we had the use of ponies for those who chose to ride. As I presume A LADY is chiefly anxious to know whether sufficient outdoor exercise is taken, I can only say that we enjoyed more than is generally allowed in English schools. Any further information that I can give is heartily at the service of the enquirer.

That stays were worn by boys after the age of breeching is confirmed incidentally by two letters printed shortly after the above, the second from M.C., who said that she was a staymaker.

                                            June 1868 (p. 326).
MAUD ELIZABETH will be glad if any correspondent will tell her the best method of fastening little boy's stockings up when they wear knickerbocker suits. MAUD ELIZABETH has tried all kinds of garters without success. Her boy is eight

years old, and his stockings are always loose upon his legs—in fact, they are constantly coming down, which gives him a most slovenly appearance. (Tie to the stays with tapes passed through loops sewn to the stockings).[1]

August 1868 (p. 112).

M.C. writes: . . . I can also inform A WIDOWER that my son was fitted with stays when seven years of age, and that he continues to wear them now that he is married.

Letters about corporal punishment started in a mild way in March 1867, but by 1869 got out of hand. So many letters were received that the publishers, Ward, Lock and Tyler, issued monthly Supplements from April to December 1870 to accommodate them. These Supplements were then collected into a volume described on its front cover: *Letters Addressed to the Editor of The Englishwoman's Domestic Magazine on The Whipping of Girls and the General Corporal Punishment of Children*, price 2 shillings. It is amusing that Ward, Lock and Tyler give their address, Warwick House, Paternoster Row, at the bottom of the cover, but omit their name. It is also worth pointing out that many of the letters are verbose and tedious in the extreme. Some of the letters of course were about the punishment of boys. One such, from 'A Rejoicer in the Restoration of the Rod' was printed in the magazine itself in March 1870. The writer described with considerable enthusiasm the birching of a boy of fifteen by two schoolmistresses in Kentish Town.

This letter provoked strong criticism, notably from 'Etonensis.' In place of corporal punishment he advocated love and shame: love had been inspired by a kindly master at Eton, shame by his sisters' governess. Before going to Eton he had been taught at home for a long time by the governess of his two sisters, one older, the other younger, than him. At the age of about eleven the governess gave him a severe whipping for not knowing a lesson in geography. This punishment having failed to produce the desired result, the governess suddenly decided to dress him in his elder sister's clothes, and with the help of the maid she succeeded in doing so. He was made to join his sisters for dinner so dressed and to remain in the clothes until he had repeated the lesson.

Supplement, April 1870.

I think Miss.....'s friend, A REJOICER IN THE RESTORATION OF THE ROD, not at all to her advantage, for surely a boy of fifteen years is rather old for such treatment from a lady. I should pity him, if I did not think little of a boy who would PERMIT a lady to do it. But sir, without entering into the matter of its efficacy to subdue, I would ask if ladies are not too severe with their birch? I was myself at Eton, and often got it there both in upper and lower school. Four cuts was the usual number, and once I got twelve with two birches, which was very sharp work; and yet I recall to memory my days with the governess at home, and remember to have often felt nearly as much. As for the usual four cuts, hers were so much worse that I did not mind it. Fancy, then, twenty cuts, as a lady writes she gave her daughter! Now, sir, I believe, that to a girl or boy of any age the sting of the punishment lies in the shame, not in the birch, and the constraining influence can also be obtained by love. If I do not take up too much space, I will prove it. I was always very idle, and could never withstand temptation. At Eton I used always on fine days to 'shirk my tutor', and get 'switched' for it, and I cared little about it. One day I was overtaken by my tutor (late Mr. Pickering) before I could help myself. He at once began to talk kindly, and after complimenting me on my abilities, he said, 'I will not again complain of you' (which meant get you whipped), but come and we will be friends'. I never again while at Eton shirked him. So much for love. I did love him. Now for shame. I was a long time taught at home by the governess of my sisters, of whom one was a little older, the other younger by two years. I was idle—perhaps more so that I was delicate. She used for this to whip me very

28

often and the whippings increased as I increased. I was between ten and eleven years of age at this time, and I used to fight for it, so that it was hard work for her and the maid of my sisters to manage it. One day I had been whipped as usual for a lesson in Geography (I remember it as if yesterday), and had fought hard, so that when the maid left I was not allowed to button up, but was made to stand with my trousers about my feet. I had thus stood for about half an hour when Miss Brock (she is dead now) demanded my lesson. I knew less about it than before. She said I should learn it, and sent me back to do so. I suppose she saw I did not look as if I was trying, and suddenly she went to the door, rang the upstairs bell, and came back. When the maid Jane came in, she said: 'Oh, Jane, I fear master N. will catch cold. Will you bring down some of Miss .....'s (my eldest sister who was about my size) clothing? Bring frock and all.' The maid lingered a moment and went. In a very few minutes back she came with the dress on her arm and her hands full. I felt as if I would sooner be killed. The governess got up, and the maid having left her clothing on the table, all but the chemise, a most desperate fight began, which lasted amidst smacks and boxes on the ears, till tired out, the garment was put on all right. Stays were easy, but now came the fight again. The first petticoat I clutched hold of, and I think for ten minutes I held on, till at last that too was accomplished and I sat on the floor enthroned in flannel. They now easily accomplished the rest; shame overcame my courage, and I had no strength. My trousers were now entirely removed. I was made to stand up, under more slaps and thumpings and threatenings of birch, while my dressing was most leisurely completed with a stiff starched petticoat, a blue frock down nearly to my feet, stockings and sandal shoes. Then I was left in my place, with my book as before. At dinner I was forced to join them; I was kept at home while they were out walking; and not until I had repeated my lesson, after the usual bedtime, was I taken upstairs to be undressed. I know not if this punishment is not more cruel than the birch; this I do know, that it put an end to it at home. The mere threat, the 'shall I send for some petticoats for you?'–always set me to work. Certainly for the governess it was, if a more tedious, at best a more feminine punishment than is the infliction of the birch by Miss..... on a boy of fifteen or even twelve. A young lady might equally dislike the garments of her brother.

ETONENSIS.

The difficulty with letters of this sort is not so much their anonymity, which, by concealing the identity, permitted the frankness, of a correspondent, but rather their indeterminacy as to date. These writers often give no indication of their present age or how long ago the alleged events took place. 'Etonensis' could be eighty in 1870 and his envelopment in petticoats might have happened at the turn of the century. Fortunately in this case 'Etonensis' has given us a link to the outside world. He tells us that his tutor at Eton was a Mr. Pickering. Now there was a master at Eton by the name of Pickering, namely Edward Hayes Pickering, assistant master from 1830 to 1852.[2] If this identification is correct, it means that this boy was dressed in his sister's clothes sometime in the second quarter of the nineteenth century, or, roughly at the beginning of the Victorian period. It is certainly the earliest example of the punishment I have come across.

The situation of 'Etonensis' in the home was not unusual for that time among the upper middle or upper classes. It is an affluent household supported by an ample staff. Before going to Eton he is educated at home with his two sisters, who seem to have their own maid as well as a governess. There is no mention of his parents, who may be abroad or unable to spend much time in the nursery. In any case there is no redress against the merciless whippings of the governess. He is surrounded by girls and women and he is finally brought to heel by the threat of being dressed in his sister's clothes whenever he misbehaves.

Of 'Etonensis' we only know that he was at Eton between the years 1830 and 1852. The experiences of another Etonian a little later go some way to corroborate or validate the letter from 'Etonensis'. The famous Lord Curzon was not dressed as a girl in childhood but he was made to wear a petticoat as a penitential garment. George Nathaniel Curzon, the eldest son of the fourth Lord Scarsdale, was born at Kedleston on January 11 1859. He was one of eleven children, the eldest being Sophia, born in 1857. The first and last Marquess Curzon of Kedleston, as he became, formerly Viceroy of India and Foreign Secretary, died on March 9, 1925. Curzon did not write an autobiography, but among his voluminous papers he left a number of autobiographical notes which his biographers have been able to use.[3] Several of these are contained in a folder described as follows in the Handlist for The Curzon Papers: 'Notes by Curzon on his early Life and Education, on his family history and on the whereabouts of MSS at Kedleston'.[4] Among these notes is a separate item headed 'School-Room Days', written in pencil on five sides of two sheets folded in half. This is a graphic account of the life of Curzon and his brothers and sisters under the tyranny of a governess, Miss Paraman, who equals or exceeds in cruelty anyone described in the pages of *The Englishwoman's Domestic Magazine* or indeed of any other paper specialising in correspondence about corporal punishment. No editor would have dared to print such cruelties had he received them in the post from a reader. Since a recent biographer, Nayana Goradia, has questioned the truth or validity of this account I will give it in full, something not so far done.

SCHOOL-ROOM DAYS

I have no particular recollection of how I fared in the first days of nursery-governess tuition. Teaching days really began for us at home (I [a word or two illegible] my sister Sophy and me also were nearly of an age and were brought up together) on the appearance on the scene of Miss P. M. Paraman in 1866 or 7. [It was 1866 according to his own diary.[5]] This remarkable woman controlled the first five of our family for over 10 years and left on all of us a mark which has never been effaced. She was a good teacher, even for subjects such as French and music, of which she knew nothing herself. In her ordinary and sensible moments she was devotedly attached to us, and continued to be so until she died in 1892, when I went and stood by her grave. She taught us good habits, economy, neatness, method, and a dislike of anything vulgar or fast. But in her savage moments she was a brutal and vindictive tyrant and I have often thought since that she must have been insane. She persecuted and beat us in the most cruel way and established over us a system of terrorism so complete that not one of us ever mustered up the courage to walk upstairs and tell our father or mother. She spanked us with the sole of her slipper on the bare back, beat us with her brushes, tied us for long hours to chairs in uncomfortable positions with our hands holding a pole or a backboard behind our backs, shut us up in darkness, practised on us every kind of petty persecution, wounded our pride by dressing us (me in particular) in red shining calico petticoats (I was obliged to make my own) with an immense conical cap on our heads round which, as well as on our breasts and back, were sewn strips of paper bearing in enormous characters, written by ourselves the words Liar Sneak Coward Lubber and the like. In this guise she compelled us to go out in the pleasure ground and show ourselves to the gardeners. She forced us to walk through the park at even distances, never communicating with each other–to the village and to show ourselves to the villagers. It never occurred to us that these good folk sympathized intensely with us and regarded her as a fiend. Our pride was much too deeply hurt. She made me write a letter to the butler asking him to make a birch for me with which I was to be punished for lying–and requesting him to read it out in the Servants'- Hall. When he came one day with a letter and saw me standing in my red petticoat with my face to the wall on a chair outside the schoolroom and said 'Why, you look like a Cardinal', I could have died of shame. She made us trundle our hoops as young children all alone up and down a place in the grounds near the hermitage where were tall black fir trees and a general air of gloom and of which we were intensely afraid. She forced us to confess to lies we had never told, to sins which we had never committed, and then punished us savagely, as being self-condemned. For weeks we were not allowed to speak to each other or to a human soul. At meal times she took all the dainties for herself and gave us nothing but tapioca and rice which we detested and which we used to drop into our laps when she was not looking and carry away and hide in chinks in the wall where she was not likely to discover them. I suppose no children well born and well placed ever cried so much or so justly.

And yet the good woman was devoted to us I believe there can be no doubt. She was especially proud of me and was always wanting me to go and see her during her illnesses in later life. To my sister Sophy she left what little money she had in the world. To others she always spoke of us as models of every virtue. I look back upon her as one of the most extraordinary phenomena I have ever encountered. She represented a class of governess and a method of tuition (in entire independence of the parents) which have both disappeared. With children who are constantly with their parents such a system would be incapable of concealment. I must say for all of us that I believe we honestly forgave her for the misery she had caused us. Not one of us ever reproached her with the past and I believe that had it been recalled to her own memory she would have dismissed it as a baseless and wicked fabrication.

As with 'Etonensis' we have a governess exercising absolute dominion over a group of children. In this case we know that the parents were on the premises, but they knew nothing of what was going on and the children were too frightened to tell them. Miss Paraman joined the family in 1866, when Curzon was seven. Curzon went to a prep school in May 1869, so he was under the sole charge of Miss Paraman for three years. Miss Paraman applied both methods of punishment in full measure. She used corporal and physical punishment of the most vicious kind. She was also an expert in shaming her victims, employing foolscaps and placards of the David Copperfield type. Curzon was not made to wear his elder sister's clothes, but he had to make and sew for himself a girl's garment, a petticoat of shining red calico, no doubt to make it as conspicuous as possible. Since he looked like a Cardinal in it, presumably it came down to his feet. But Miss Paraman realised that the essential element in making a child feel ashamed is the exposure to witnesses. It was bad enough for 'Etonensis' in his girl's frock to have to sit at table with his sisters and governess and be seen by the maids, but Curzon and his siblings were forced to walk about outside in their humiliating garb and show themselves to the servants, gardeners and villagers.

There are curious similarities between the anonymous letter of 'Etonensis' and Curzon's note. Both achieve a similar end, namely confession or revelation. As a famous man, Curzon knows that his manuscript reminiscences will become known and possibly be published after his death. Before that they are confidential and private, but he has recorded the most deeply felt humiliations of his childhood. 'Etonensis' cannot rely on this. The anonymous letter gives him the opportunity to confess, to reveal his shame, but retain his privacy. Both accounts describe the cruel and ruthless punishment of a boy by a woman in authority. In both, but especially in Curzon's, there is the implication that the woman enjoyed making the boy wear petticoats. Whether this was the case or not, a malicious pleasure in the situation is ascribed to the woman. Curzon's phrases, 'wounded our pride by dressing us (me in particular) in red shining red calico petticoats (I was obliged to make my own)' evoke amazingly well Curzon's own shame and Miss Paraman's supposed pleasure in creating it.

There are three incidents in, or aspects of, Curzon's later life which are relevant to mention here, as echoing in some way Miss Paraman's treatment of him or as falling within the subject of boys in stays. As a boy Curzon had suffered several accidents, in particular a fall from a horse when he was fifteen. Just before going up to Balliol in October 1878 he was diagnosed as having curvature of the spine and was obliged thereafter to wear an orthopaedic corset, an appliance of canvas and steel into which he was fastened like someone under the regime of the

CORSAGE DE DESSOUS POUR PETITE FILLE
DE DIX A DOUZE ANS.

PANTALON POUR PETITE FILLE DE TROIS A CINQ ANS.

PANTALON POUR PETIT GARÇON DE DEUX A QUATRE ANS.

CORSAGE DE DESSOUS POUR ENFANT
DE TROIS A CINQ ANS.

PANTALON POUR PETITE FILLE DE DIX A DOUZE ANS.

6. Children's Underwear.

La Mode Illustrée, 1867 (pp. 354-5).

stay-lace. [6]

While Curzon was at Oxford the celebrated verse was composed about him:

> My name is George Nathaniel Curzon,
> I am a most superior person,
> My cheek is pink, my hair is sleek,
> I dine at Blenheim once a week.

It was true of course that he did dine occasionally with the Duke and Duchess of Marlborough. Kenneth Rose tells of an occasion when the dinner party went on so long that he was asked to stay the night and having no luggage was accommodated with a nightgown belonging to Lady Randolph Churchill.[7] Unfortunately the reference Rose gave in the first edition was incorrect. This was, however, put right in the paperback version of 1985, so I now quote the original narrative from the *Reminiscences* of Grace Curzon, Curzon's second wife.

> Writing of her [Jenny, Lady Randolph Churchill] reminds me of a story that George used often to tell of himself in his Balliol days. It will be remembered that the undergraduate verse which dogged him to the end of his days concluded with the line: 'I dine at Blenheim once a week.' George used to relate how on one of those occasions at Blenheim the party went on so long that he was asked to stay the night. Of course he had brought no luggage with him, and so, by way of night-clothes, he was provided with one of Lady Randolph Churchill's nightdresses to sleep in. (Those were, of course, the days of nightshirts, before pyjamas had been invented, and so perhaps the contrast was not so great as it would have been for a man accustomed to pyjamas. Still, George used to say that he had felt rather ridiculous in it.)[8]

One wonders whether this was a sort of practical joke engineered by the ladies of the party, as surely there would have been a male nightshirt somewhere about, the Duke's for instance? One also imagines that Lady Randolph's nightdress would have been made of fine lawn and much bedecked with lace. It is curiously analogous to the petticoat imposed by Miss Paraman. Lady Randolph does not mention the incident in her own memoirs, but she does make this revealing comment about her mother-in-law, Frances Anne, Duchess of Marlborough (1822-99), who would, I believe, also have been present at the dinner party mentioned: 'She ruled Blenheim and nearly all those in it with a firm hand. At the rustle of her silk dress the household trembled.'[9] According to Curzon's daughter Irene, Miss Paraman wore 'long, voluminous skirts edged with braid'.[10] That would of course have been in accordance with the fashion of the time, but it is nice to have a statement to that effect.

The third incident I wish to mention here is something reported by Curzon of the cruelty of Abdur Rahman, the Emir of Afghanistan (1844-1901). In 1894 Curzon visited Kabul as a private citizen. The Emir told him of many ruthless punishments he had inflicted on his subjects.

> Another incident happened soon after I left Kabul, the victim of which was an officer whom I had seen daily during my visits to the Palace. This was a dapper little figure, the Commandant of the Amir's Bodyguard, who was always in attendance, in a beautiful uniform, in the Durbar Hall. He had, when a boy, been one of the Amir's favourite *batchas* or dancing-boys (an amusement much favoured in Afghanistan), and when his master attained to power, he had been promoted stage by stage until he had reached his present eminence.
>
> This man was believed, or found, to be guilty of some act of disloyalty or treachery to his Sovereign, and the latter heard of it before the culprit discovered that he had been detected. The scene happened in full Durbar, when one day the Amir told the story of the culprit's guilt, while he stood before him in his brilliant uniform, and thus announced the punishment:
>
> 'A *batcha* you began and a *batcha* you shall end. Go back to your house and take off your uniform and put on your petticoats (the dancing-boys in Afghanistan dance in petticoats), and come back and dance here before the Durbar.'

The wretched man, a general, and forty years of age, had to do as he was bidden, and to come and dance in the garb of a girl before the assembled Court of Kabul. Can anything more refined in its cruelty be imagined?[11]

As someone who had worn a red petticoat in the presence of the servants, Curzon was particularly well qualified to judge of this cruelty. I have already mentioned that Nayana Goradia casts doubt on the credibility of Curzon's narrative.[12] She writes that Kenneth Rose first aroused her suspicions about the Miss Paraman episode and that he had reached a blind alley in trying to trace Miss Paraman's background.[13] I see no reason to doubt Curzon's own words which carry complete conviction. I accept that Lady Scarsdale loved her children, but that does not mean that she could not have given Miss Paraman a free hand in the school-room.

Fortunately important new information has come to light. When Curzon's latest biographer, David Gilmour, started work, Mr David Yates Mason, Miss Paraman's great-great-nephew, wrote to him about the family. He has now kindly given me some more information.[14] Miss Ellen Mary Paraman (1826-1892) had four sisters and a brother, the youngest. Their father was Robert Paraman, Governor of Norwich City Gaol from at least 1836 to 1842 when he died. He made his children watch executions, which were of course then carried out in public. Two of her sisters were governesses in Norfolk families. A third taught at a school described in *Kelly's Directory for Cambs., Norfolk and Suffolk for 1858* as a 'preparatory school for young gentlemen, Bellevue House, Pottergate Street', owned by Mrs Henry R. Priest, whose husband was a partner in Priest & Pilgrim, wine merchants, 1, St. Giles Street. In the same Directory Robert Paraman's widow, Christiana, is shown as conducting a milliners' business with a fourth daughter, Rosa, at 56, St. Giles Street. Mr Mason writes: 'The Paraman aunts were legendary dragons in my mother's family the one exception being Rosa, my great-grandmother, who was happily married. Though only a child when she died my mother retained the most vivid memories of her.'

Gilmour now reveals there is a portrait of the schoolmistress, Miss Eliza Paraman, in a novel by the Norfolk writer, Mrs Mary E. Mann (1848-1929), *The Memories of Ronald Love* published in 1907. Either the school was notorious for the cruel punishments inflicted on the pupils by Miss Paraman or this was known personally to Mrs Mann. The names are hardly changed at all. The school is a 'Seminary for Young Gentlemen' (p. 58) at 'Belle Vue House' (p. 92). Mrs Priest becomes 'Mrs Priestley', Miss Eliza Paraman 'Miss Eliza Pergaman', while 'Mr Priestley' is a wine merchant (p. 76).

Ronald is a boy of six, the natural son of a doctor in Norwich who has not married but merely visits the boy's mother. When the latter marries someone of her own class, Ronald is sent to a small private school for little boys. The year is 1850. The school is owned and run by a Mrs Priestley, but the chief mistress is a 'Miss Pergaman,' who subjects the boys to a variety of cruel punishments. No boy is made to wear a petticoat but they are made to lie under her chair for fidgeting and she beats them with her hairbrush or stay-busk. The novel is painful in the extreme to read, but Ronald's first experience of the school-room validates to some extent Curzon's account of his Miss Paraman.

> If anyone had asked him the number of the boys assembled there he would have said a hundred, that being the figure by which he was accustomed to express any assemblage of units beyond two. In fact, there were twenty-five besides himself; they sat each on his own little box of books, five deep, and five in a line. Those sat who were not in class, at the writing-shelf, at Mrs Priestley's desk, or under punishment, that is. One stood on his box, a dunce's cap on his head, and round his neck a placard, with which Ronald was to make close acquaintance later, announcing in boldly-written characters–'I am a bad boy.' Another, beneath one of the high windows (the school-room was an attic, merely, and all the three windows were in the roof) occupied the piece of furniture afterwards introduced to the new boy's unwilling notice as 'the stocks.' This was merely a plank of wood bordered on each side with low walls,

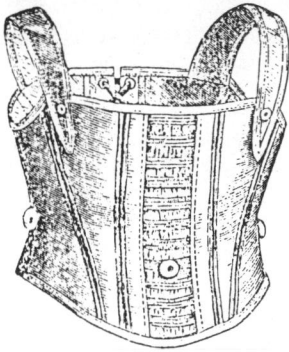

CORSET POUR ENFANT
DE DEUX A QUATRE ANS.

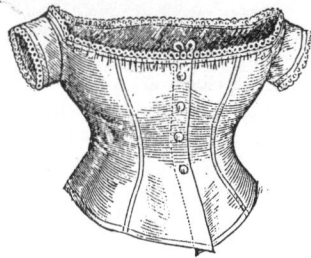

CORSAGE DE DESSOUS POUR
PETITE FILLE DE 8 A 10 ANS.

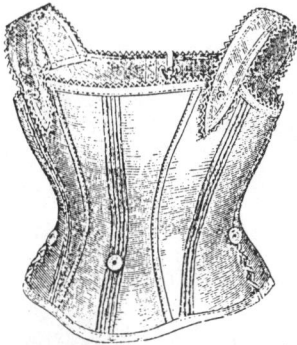

CORSET POUR PETITE FILLE DE 8 A 10 ANS.
(52 centimètres de tour de taille.)

CHEMISE POUR FILLETTE DE TREIZE A QUINZE ANS.

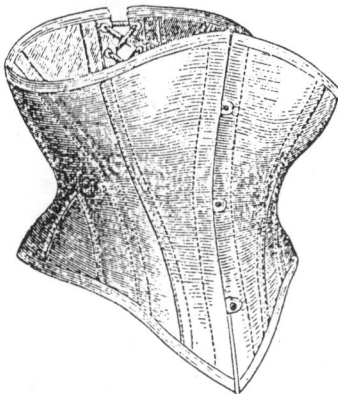

CORSET POUR JEUNE FILLE.
(50 centimètres de tour de taille.)

PANTALON POUR PETITE FILLE DE 8 A 10 ANS.

7. Children's Underwear.   *La Mode Illustrée*, 1872 (pp. 226 and 382).

at that uncomfortable angle known at the dancing academies of the time as the 'first position.' What good was supposed to accrue to the rising generation from that unnatural and uneasy attitude, Mrs Priestley could not have said. It was sufficient for her purpose that it was extremely uncomfortable, perhaps.

Yet another pupil, undergoing chastisement, lay on his back beneath Miss Pergaman's chair; his narrow body squeezed in between its back and front legs, his arms as in a vice at his sides; his head and feet protruded beyond the lady's skirts, and his eyes were fixed on the raftered ceiling. This was a favourite method of enforcing quietude on restless boys. The space beneath the chair was seldom unoccupied. One or other of the children had always fidgeted with hands or feet in a fashion to qualify him for the painful position.

Before the half-hour's instruction bestowed on him by his fellow-pupil (an advanced scholar himself, into words of two syllables, and of the mature age of eight) was over, yet another young gentleman, more culpable than the rest, was led off by Miss Pergaman to her bedroom. In the retirement of that chaste seclusion she was in the habit of administering corporeal punishment on slight provocation and with no sparing hand.

For this ceremonial she had a choice of weapons. Owing to the position he was compelled to assume the small malefactor was in uncertainty until the first stroke was received as to whether he was being assaulted by her hairbrush or the busk of her stays. . . . When Miss Pergaman returned, a little heated from her exertions but unaccompanied–the object of her educational energy having been sent to bed on a diet of bread and water for the rest of the day–she found all in their places.[15]

In later issues of the Supplement there were two references to the letter signed by 'Etonensis,' one highly critical and the other favourable. 'G.H.D.' wrote several letters to the Editor, deploring and denouncing the practice of whipping both boys and girls. This is his comment on the letter from 'Etonensis.'

Supplement, August 1870.
ETONENSIS presents us with another edifying picture of the outrages committed by a governess and maid upon a boy of ten or eleven years of age. He seems to think that the last method he describes was more 'feminine' than birching. I hope, for the honour of women, it was not, accompanied as the performance was by both violence and indecency. What is so detestable in these matters is the hypocrisy. Brothels do not put up for schools of virtue; but these women are not ashamed to pretend that these revolting outrages are for the good of the victim, and in the cause of good behaviour, while they are only too often committed to gratify their lustful desires.   G.H.D.

The last remark refers to the lady correspondents who described approvingly episodes of corporal punishment. It is interesting that at this date 'G.H.D.' sees a sexual motive and gratification in the governess dressing a boy as a girl. 'Philalethia' (lover of truth), on the other hand, thinks her methods should be given a try. This correspondent contributed many long, eloquent letters in favour of the corporal punishment of boys and girls. There is at least one in almost every issue of the Supplement, some several columns long. The following comes in the middle of a very long letter.

Supplement, September 1870.
I wish now to speak of the April paper by ETONENSIS as I find it has been passed over [presumably written before he received the August Supplement]. Whoever introduces a new drug into a pharmacopoeia is worthy of some consideration, especially if the slightest experience of its efficacy is brought forward. I pass over the first part of

his paper as to my mind altogether untenable; it is ridiculous to say that a lady cannot effectually contend with a boy of fifteen, and cannot produce most salutary effects by compelling him to submit to her; there are far too many cases of the contrary to allow what ETONENSIS says on this head to pass. . . . . My object is to speak of the method which ETONENSIS proposes as a substitute for the rod–viz. to array naughty girls in coat, waistcoat, trousers, shirt and necktie; and naughty boys in frock, stays, petticoat, chemise and perhaps a cap. He thinks that the scheme thus caused would be quite sufficient to produce submission to authority, and says that for himself the words 'shall I send for some petticoats for you?' always set him to work. Now this is a new idea and may be worth considering, though if what he says about non-submission be thought by any to be worth anything, the punishment which he proposes would appear to these people as even more difficult to manage than a mere whipping would be. The process for a naughty boy indeed would perhaps be comparatively easy; frock, petticoat, and chemise may be slipped over the head, but to force a naughty girl's legs, if she be turbulent, into a pair of trousers would be found to be very difficult, and would involve a scuffle very offensive, I fear, to supersentimentalists; and I am afraid too that the lofty defenders of the honour of boys would consider it an inexpiable injury, to array them in a frock, petticoat and chemise. FANNY AND ME [two girls who, according to the letter from one of them, subjected their governess to corporal punishment] are I suppose myths, but if that history be real, it would require, I suspect, the energy of two or three 'Miss Stick-ups' [the chastised governess] to array those damsels like boys. Still the proposal of ETONENSIS banishes pain from chastisement, and may be worth a trial. Cannot someone make the experiment? It would give some small impetus to trade, as suits of the proper clothes of more than one size must be kept in readiness at all schools and in many families. I hardly think that ALICE de V. and the rest of the TINY club [opponents of corporal punishment] will favour the plan of ETONENSIS; they will be horrified at the inevitable exposure, and I can understand some saying that thus to force naughty boys to wear the dress of girls will accustom them to the notion, and may bring on more pranks like those which have been lately before the public [a clear reference to the case of Boulton and Park which was heard before the police court in April and May 1870 and was reported in the Press at great length: see my *Men in Petticoats*], and so this punishment will be declaimed against as immoral. I, indeed, should not think of arguing thus; to me it is perfectly ridiculous to say that chastisement teaches either girls or boys to be immodest if it is accompanied by an exposure; the said exposure will, of course, be associated with chastisement, which is a disagreeable thing, and nothing is in general rendered attractive by being associated with what is disagreeable. The theory of ETONENSIS should, however, be investigated as I said before.   PHILALETHIA.

This letter continued for two or three more columns and illustrates the serious and copious manner in which these matters were discussed. 'Philalethia' gave the information that he had not gone to Eton, but was an Oxford graduate. He once gave his address as 5, York Terrace, Queenstown. It is interesting that he had not heard of the punishment inflicted on 'Etonensis.' This suggests that it was a new idea for punishment at the time. In the October Supplement 'Philalethia' gave a long account of the experiences of a boy who was educated at a girls' school as a 'parlour boarder' while his parents were in India. At the age of fifteen he was birched by the head governess 'who was a beautiful and accomplished young lady of twenty-two'. He was made to take off his trousers, jacket and waistcoat and lie across her lap.

Supplement, October 1870.
    She placed herself on a high chair and her feet on a footstool, so as to make a broad lap. She desired me to lie across it well spread . . . I forgot to mention that on

each time upon being flogged by her–perhaps to strike awe–she tied on a punishment apron of black satin. Her own dress she lifted up in front, and tied the black apron over it, all in silence. . PHILALETHIA.

This is an example of the punisher wearing a punishment costume. It also illustrates the common case of a boy left in England to be educated while his parents were abroad. The special Supplement for letters about punishment finished in December 1870. A few more such letters appeared in the 'Conversazione' up to November 1873. The last letter about corsets was printed in December 1873. Mrs. Mathilda Browne ('Silkworm') left the magazine at the end of 1874 to start her own magazine, *Myra's Journal* while Beeton himself died on 6 June 1877. The magazine changed its name to *The Illustrated Household Journal and Englishwoman's Domestic Magazine* from January 1880 and in 1881 was incorporated in *The Milliner, Dressmaker, and Draper*, but that ran for only six issues. In view of the references to 'stocks' in Mary Mann's novel quoted above and in *The Family Doctor* in chapter V, I will include one final letter from this magazine.

THE STOCKS   JUNE 1879 (p. 330).
    TERPSICHORE writes: I have seen in the ENGLISHWOMAN'S DOMESTIC MAGAZINE for January a letter signed STOCKS, in which inquiry is made regarding the instrument of that name used for correcting the habit so common in young people of turning in the toes. I am sorry to hear that, owing to some stupid prejudice, this useful instrument, so much used in Continental schools, should have fallen into disuse in England. I cannot believe that the 'stocks' has ever done injury when used with proper judgment. The patient should be taught to refrain from shuffling her feet about in order to get rid of the feeling of restraint, and if she cannot be persuaded to do this the ankles should be tied or strapped together. There will then be no danger of the joint becoming enlarged or too prominent. The best description of stocks I have seen was that used in a large school in Italy, and was constructed as follows: On a flat mahogany board were fastened, so as to form a very broad letter V, four strips of wood about an inch high. The feet being placed in the grooves thus formed would remain turned out at an angle of about 100 degrees, with the heels touching them, but the strips of wood, turning upon pivots at the apex of the angle, after the manner of compasses, could be further turned back till the feet formed one straight line, the strips of wood being kept steady by means of pegs driven into holes placed at regular intervals. The advantage of this plan is obvious. The feet, instead of being turned out in a straight line from the first, or always kept at the same angle, are gradually educated till they can be turned out without difficulty or excessive pain to the person who employs them. I think the 'stocks' should be used in all schools and families. Even in the case of little boys they may often be used with advantage; and they should also be used by adults who have contracted an inveterate habit of turning in the toes. Experience convinces me that no amount of drill or dancing lessons will avail to correct this ungainly trick, so common amongst English girls, when once it has become inveterate. The much-abused stocks, on the contrary, never fail to do good. They are, moreover, very useful as a punishment, but if the feet are to be turned out at an angle of more than 100 degrees they should not be kept in durance vile for more than an hour at a time. The 'stocks' should be employed both sitting and standing, and occasionally accompanied by the backboard and collar. These latter instruments, when used with moderation and judgment, are also very useful, though they have, probably through the fault of careless governesses, been made the subject of much undeserved abuse, and I rejoice to learn from your correspondent that they are again coming into fashion. In these days there is a great deal too much of that false benevolence which sees cruelty in every kind of discipline. Girls generally learn to like the use of instruments like those above

described, and the pain and inconvenience which undoubtedly accompany their use at first is soon submitted to with fortitude, and even pleasure. I may as well observe that when the feet are turned out in line, or nearly so, the patient should stand with her back against the wall, so as not to lose her balance, head erect, and arms straight down by her sides; or she may, when placed in the stocks for punishment, stand with her face against the wall. She should also be occasionally made to perform the exercise known in dancing as *les pliés*, with her feet in the stocks, and then to walk up and down for half-an-hour or so with the backboard on.

1   An engraving in *The Young Ladies' Journal* of 1878 shows a child's stockings suspendered from a shirt (vol. 15, p. 376.)
2   H.E.C. Stapylton, *The Eton School Lists* (London, 1864), p. x.
3   The Earl of Ronaldshay, *The Life of Lord Curzon* (London: Ernest Benn, 1928), I, 17-18; Leonard Mosley, *Curzon, The End of an Epoch* (London: Longmans, 1960), pp. 7-10; Kenneth Rose, *Curzon: A Most Superior Person* (London: Macmillan, 1969), pp. 19-21; Nayana Goradia, *Lord Curzon, The Last of the British Moghuls* (Delhi: OUP, 1993), pp. 43-9; David Gilmour, *Curzon* (London: John Murray, 1994), pp. 7-9 See also Jonathan Gathorne-Hardy, *The Rise and Fall of the British Nanny* (London: Hodder & Stoughton, 1972), pp. 302-09.
4   MSS EUR F. 112/363 in the Oriental and India Office Collections of the British Library, 197, Blackfriars Road, London, SE1 8NG.
5   Nayana Goradia, op. cit., p. 43.
6   K. Rose, op. cit., pp. 45-7; N. Goradia, op. cit., pp. 66-99 and 197.
7   K. Rose, op. cit., p. 49.
8   Grace Curzon, The Marchioness Curzon of Kedleston, *Reminiscences* (London: Hutchinsons, 1955), p. 30.
9   Mrs. George Cornwallis-West, *The Reminiscences of Lady Randolph Churchill* (London: Edward Arnold, 1908), p. 61. See also *The Complete Peerage* (London, 1932), VIII, 503.
10   Baroness Ravensdale, *Little Innocents: Childhood Reminiscences* (London, 1932), p. 10, quoted by Nayana Goradia, op. cit., p. 43.
11   Marquess Curzon of Kedleston, *Tales of Travel* (London: Hodder and Stoughton, 1923), pp. 77-8.
12   Nayana Goradia, op. cit., pp. 48-9 and 268. Incidentally, the notes headed "School-Room Days" are not written on notepaper stamped with the address, 1, Carlton House Terrace, although Goradia may be right about the date they were written.
13   Nayana Goradia, op. cit., pp. 48 and 268.
14   David Gilmour, op.cit., p. 8.
15   Mary E. Mann, *The Memories of Ronald Love* (London: Methuen, 1907), pp. 65-8.

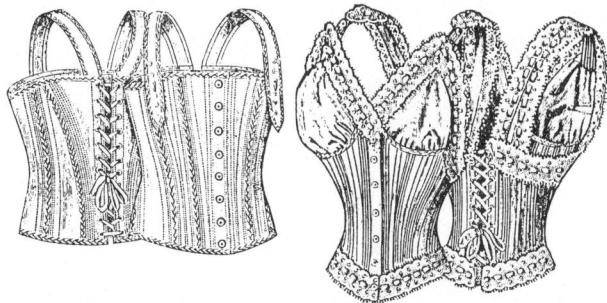

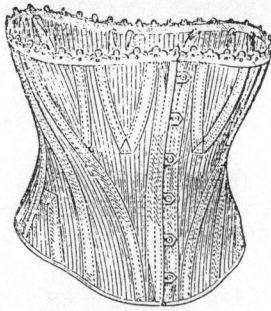

CORSET POUR FILLETTE
DE 11 A 13 ANS (DEVANT).

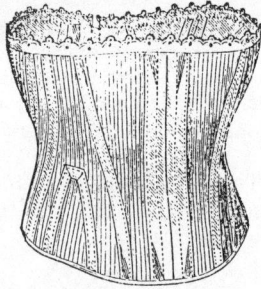

CORSET POUR FILLETTE
DE 11 A 13 ANS (DOS).

CHEMISE POUR PETITE FILLE
DE 6 A 8 ANS.

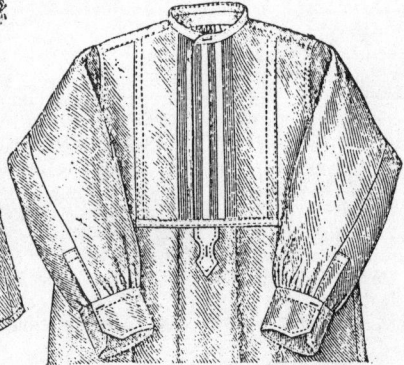

CHEMISE DE JOUR POUR PETIT GARÇON
DE 6 A 8 ANS.

PANTALON POUR PETITE FILLE DE 8 A 10 ANS.

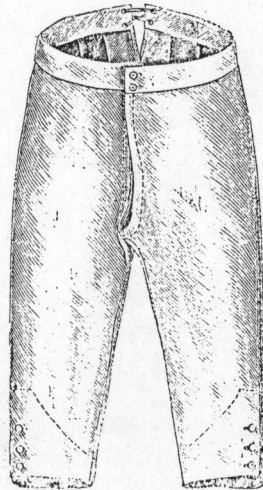

CALEÇON POUR PETIT GARÇON
DE 8 A 10 ANS.

8. Children's Underwear.

La Mode Illustrée, 1876 (pp. 267 and 371)

IV
TOWN TALK

Town Talk was founded by Adolphus Rosenberg as a 'Journal for Society at Large' on Saturday, 16 November 1878. His special interests were suggestive society gossip and the exposure and denunciation of vice and indecency. An example of the former is: 'The Countess is having a baby–how are they going to name it?–surely not after the Earl?' On 23 November 1878 there was an article entitled 'In a Disorderly House by A Victim'. The following year Rosenberg achieved fame by attacking Lillie Langtry in his gossip column. After various references to her, he claimed on 30 August 1879 that Mr. Langtry had filed a petition for divorce with The Prince of Wales and two others as co-respondents. At first there was no response, and Rosenberg asserted on 4 October 1879 that the petition had been withdrawn. When, however, William Cornwallis-West sued Rosenberg for some distasteful remarks about his wife on the same date, Mr. and Mrs. Langtry brought their own case against him and Rosenberg was sent to prison for eighteen months for defamatory libel[1].

The paper lingered on until 10 April 1880, and that ended its first series. When Rosenberg came out of prison, he immediately started the paper up again on 14 May 1881. One of the topics which excited Rosenberg's wrath was 'indecent whipping', by which he meant the whipping of children by members of the opposite sex. There were articles and letters from readers on this subject. Rosenberg sometimes repeated articles and letters from previous issues and he also copied letters which had appeared in *The Family Herald* and in *The Englishwoman's Domestic Magazine*. One in particular, on 12 May 1883, was the letter from 'Etonensis' reproduced above from the Supplement of April 1870. The beginning was slightly altered to omit the reference to the previous correspondent, the tutor's name was left out and the signatory was changed to 'E'. Otherwise it was the same. It produced a reply which does seem to be genuine.

26 May 1883

I (along no doubt with others) have read 'E.I.'s' intelligent and perspicuous letter with much interest.[2] If any of your readers cared to read the correspondence in a certain fashionable journal a few years ago, they would find the mode of punishment quoted in the second part of 'E.I.'s' was not so infrequent as some might imagine.

As to its efficacy, or its advantages or its disadvantages on the score of cruelty or indelicacy, I leave your readers to judge, as I have noticed not one letter appeared as a dissentient to it–all in its favour. I myself have known cases stated where a well grown boy has been compelled to submit to dress in his sister's clothing either as a punishment or preparatory to being birched, and in all cases I have heard of with the happiest results. And I agree entirely with 'E.I.'s' remark that this method, if more tedious, is at best a more feminine one than the cruelty of the birch.

Moortown Leeds.   A READER.

So far I have not been able to trace that tantalising 'certain fashionable journal', but it must belong to the period 1870 to 1883, probably just before 1880. It suggests that the use of this punishment had increased by the end of the third quarter of the nineteenth century. The next correspondent wrote about the constant use of the birch by a governess in a family of four, girls aged sixteen, thirteen and ten, and a boy of twelve. The boy was dressed as a girl to receive the birch, perhaps for reasons of modesty, but sometimes, to shame him further, he was obliged to stay so dressed.

When the governess considered it necessary to punish a girl, she took her to a room upstairs alone, placed a long soft pillow on a form and made the delinquent lie on it with her legs hanging down on either side. The ankles were then fastened together under the form and the hands in front. She then turned up the girl's clothes to her waist, exposing her just sufficiently for the infliction of a merited punishment, and birched her soundly. When the boy had to be whipped he was made to go upstairs and change his clothes for a punishment dress, which consisted of a short frock and petticoats barely reaching to his knees, stays, chemise and embroidered drawers some inches longer than the frock. The whipping was then inflicted in exactly the same manner as above described, no difference being made between boy and girls in the severity of the whipping; but the boy was sometimes further humiliated by making him remain dressed in his sister's clothes for sometime after the birching. After the first whipping the governess had no difficulty in making any of her pupils submit to their frequent punishments. I can confirm 'Housebox's' account of the whipping of girls trained for public performance. SCHILLING

The experiences of the following correspondent are similar to those described by 'Philalethia' in the October Supplement of the *E.D.M.*

INDECENT WHIPPING   15 March 1884.

I have been much interested in the correspondence upon the above subject, which you have published. Some of the practices which have come to light seem to me to be grossly indecent; but I do not think that sufficient attention has been paid to indecent punishments in boys' schools kept by ladies. I was a weak and delicate boy and was sent by my parents to a school in the suburbs kept by a lady. The school contained only fourteen small boys of ages varying from six to fourteen. I was twelve years old. The principal was a tall, thin woman, exceedingly plain but very smart in her dress. The two governesses were in awe of her and obeyed her implicitly in everything. They were not allowed to punish us in any way, but they had orders to present a report of our behaviour everyday. At twelve o'clock the principal used to enter the school room in a black or brown satin dress and take her seat for the Bible class, the only class she herself held. The governesses then read out the names of the boys on the punishment list, who were ordered to stand up. The principal then read a chapter in the Bible, after which she ordered one of the boys to fetch a whip. For slight offences during lessons she would whip the smaller boys across her knee, after removing their clothes, and the bigger boys on the palm of the hand. For graver matters, however, the delinquent was sent to the punishment room for a private whipping. Many a time have I gone through this ordeal, which took place in the following way. The principal first would order me to take off my jacket and trousers, and then I was made to kneel over a low block, covered with red satin. She would then lift up her petticoat and place her left leg over my neck and whip me slowly with a birch rod. Between every two or three strokes she admonished me, and made me promise to obey her. When this operation, which she called the correction, was over, she sat down, and I was made to kneel before her, and ordered to kiss her feet, the skirt of her dress, and the rod and then to thank her for correcting me, and to beg her to be so good as to whip me for having been so naughty. Sometimes she was not satisfied with this, and would administer a few more strokes with the birch in the same manner; but when she considered I was sufficiently subdued she turned me across her left knee and slapped me with her hand or slipper. After which she always said: 'Now join your school-fellows; the next time you are reported to me I shall whip you more severely'. I think two or three of us were whipped every day in the school room, but as only the five elder boys received private whippings, the punishment room was only used about once a fortnight.   HENRY BROWN.

The next correspondent approved of the methods of Brown's lady principal. Calling herself 'Julia,' she believed in giving a punishment a thoroughly feminine character, putting the culprit in girls' clothes afterwards.

5 July 1884

I have read with much interest the letters that have appeared recently in your valuable little paper about whipping, and having considerable experience of the employment of that punishment and of the results, I venture to make a few observations to you on the subject which I hope may appear next week.

In the first place, then, I wish to say that, as a general rule, I disapprove of girls being whipped. In certain exceptional cases, where the offence is very serious and of an indelicate kind, or where the culprit is particularly lazy or sluggish, a sound birching may not harm; but most girls, or many girls, are made vicious by the very infliction that was to improve them.

With boys up to sixteen or seventeen I have found the contrary to be the case; and so far from disapproving of their being punished in a motherly fashion by one of the other sex, I find the shame consequent upon that and from the exposure etc. to be a part of the penance very much dreaded, and an important element in its effectiveness. Thus I quite understand why one of your correspondents dressed the delinquent in his sister's clothes, and why another, after preparing him, placed her leg across his neck.

I always took care to make the operation as shameful as possible, and to give it a thoroughly feminine character, finding this to be , as I have said, most dreaded. A shy and nervous boy I always so whipped as to make him expose himself. Stripping him to his shirt, he was made to lie across a rather high bed so that his feet would scarcely touch the ground, his shirt was well fastened up all round, my maid and one of the housemaids were invariably present, and if there were any lady visitors staying in the house they would be there too, whether young or old. I never knew any ill result to them, and the shame their being witnesses caused invariably resulted well. Then, having lectured the youth for some few minutes, I began by giving a vigorous stroke or two across the legs just above the knees, the consequence invariably being that the legs were drawn violently up, or one drawn up and the other stretched out, and the boy made to act most ridiculous capers. I continued whipping his legs for some five or six minutes, gradually moving upwards, and finishing off with a determined deliberate dozen. The young gentleman was then made to don petticoats for the rest of the day, and was given specially in charge to two young ladies, if they were disposed for it, or to my maid. Of course this was quite a nominal infliction, but it involved a good deal of submission to sundry slaps, teasing, and so on, which was highly beneficial.

A great deal also depends on the manner the stripes are given. My method is to give half across and the rest along the legs, sanding for the last with my back to the boy's head.

I should be very glad to hear the opinions of some other lady correspondents upon my view of punishing, and their experience. I may say I do not invariably use a birch; a slipper or the back of a hairbrush are very good instruments, and the hand too sometimes. I am surprised that none of your correspondents have noticed an account given in one of the appendices to the 'Ride Through Asia Minor' of the treatment to travellers in Kurdestan by the women of that country.

Parties of girls are there said sometimes to waylay a traveller, drag him from his horse, and divest him of all his clothing, to then give him a slight whipping, and dance before him in their most enticing manner; that then, if he shows the least forgetfulness of propriety, he is taken to a court of matrons, who sentence him to receive a certain number of strokes, which are forthwith inflicted; after which the dancing goes on again, and probably results in another whipping, and so on for some hours.

One of your correspondents speaks of Prussian ladies being members of whipping clubs, but she need not go so far abroad. And elsewhere men are not always excluded as many of your readers must know. I should not wonder if the Eastern practices were found to exist nearer home.   JULIA

I have not been able to identify 'Ride Through Asia Minor'. Julia followed up her request for the opinions of lady readers by inserting this advertisement in the issue for 31 January 1885: 'Julia would be glad to correspond in strict confidence with some ladies about whipping. Julia c/o Mme Roccs, 2A, Hanway Street, Oxford Street, W'. The Post Office Directory for 1892 has the following entry: '2, Hanway Street: North Side: Mrs. Rose Rocca, stationer'. Hanway Street is still there on the North side of Oxford Street at the junction with Tottenham Court Road, but the buildings are of a later date. This is obviously an accommodation address, which was also used by a Mr J. Dering in *The Family Doctor* of 4 June 1892 as we shall see, although the latter gives '2, Hanway Street' as if it were his own address. In chapter 24 of George Gissing's novel, *The Odd Women*, published in 1893, Mrs Widdowson requires such an address and the narrator makes this comment: 'The receiving of letters which, for one reason or another, must be dispatched to a secret address, is a very ordinary complaisance on the part of small London stationers; hundreds of such letters are sent and called for every week within the metropolitan postal area.'

As regards 'whipping clubs', 'Julia' may be right. One such is described in *A Full and True Account of the Wonderful Mission of Earl Lavender, which lasted one night and one day: with a history of the pursuit of Earl Lavender and Lord Brumm by Mrs Scamler and Maud Emblem . . . With a frontispiece by Aubrey Beardsley* by the poet John Davidson (1857-1907) published in 1895. The male and female members of this 'club' whip each other and a special costume is provided for this purpose.

The schoolmistress complained of in the next letter made her victims wear a pair of her own drawers as if in token of having been vanquished by her.

7 February 1885.

The punishment of whipping is not in itself indecent (provided, of course, that girls are only whipped by ladies, and that boys of the age of puberty are not whipped by women), It is the way the thing is done that sometimes constitutes impropriety.

At one of our best watering places there is a boys' school kept by ladies. The boys, some eighty in number, are divided into the 'infant class' for very young children; the 'lower school' for boys from five to eight years; the 'middle school' for boys from eight to eleven; the 'senior school' for boys from eleven to fourteen; and the 'backward class' for very bad or intractable boys from twelve to fifteen.

A lady friend of mine having a very backward nephew of fourteen, sent the boy to the school, hearing that the head mistress, although a severe disciplinarian, was very successful, but the first time the youth saw his aunt, he complained of the whipping, and my friend, after examining his person, found him very much wealed, but thought he had probably deserved it. However, when the lad went into details, the aunt made enquiries which led to the nephew being removed from the school, not because of the whipping itself, but on account of some of the accessories.

The lady principal's practice is to make the elder boys kneel on a flogging block, she then undresses and prepares them herself; straps their knees firmly to the block to prevent them rising, seats herself facing their heads, and holds the boys in position by pressing her knees firmly on each side of their necks. She then birches them very slowly and securely, with a great deal of lecturing. The boy resumes his jacket and waistcoat, but instead of his own nether garments he has to don for the rest of the day a pair of his governess's prettily worked drawers of red flannel or white longcloth according to the season.   M. HOLBORNFIELDS

E. de K. suggested that it would be less indecent for an older boy to be whipped by women if he were dressed as a girl.

I quite agree with by far the greater number of your correspondents on this subject that there is no indecency in a girl being whipped as long as none of the male sex be present, but decidedly indecent if any man or boy be present. As far as I can see, it is no more indecent for a girl to expose her person to be whipped than to expose it before her bed-room companions in dressing and undressing, which she necessarily must do in a school where this kind of punishment is mostly in force, and where five or six girls sleep in the same room. if it is indecent for a girl to be whipped before the opposite sex, surely it is equally indecent for a boy to be whipped by, or in the presence of, women. Of course I mean boys of eleven and upwards, who are often kept up to that age in schools kept by ladies, and who are frequently birched when naughty. In fact it is more indecent in preparing a boy than a girl. It is generally necessary to have the assistance of a governess or maid, invariably a young woman (as few big boys will submit quietly to be flogged by a woman), and can anything be more indecent to a woman than the exhibition of a boy naked from his waist to his heels, or for the boy so to expose himself? I think no boy should be kept at a ladies' school after he is eleven years old at the latest. If by chance it should be necessary for a boy over that age to be at a ladies' school, and as there is but one punishment for grave offences for boys of this age, viz. the birch, and but one place and in one condition for its application, I think it would be better, as some of your correspondents say is done, the boy should be dressed as a girl, as the disgrace of appearing in such a dress before his schoolfellows will add to the punishment, and he will be prepared for the birch with far less indecency than dressed in his ordinary clothes. During the operations he should be so held or fastened down that there can be no struggling, and the birch should be applied with the greatest severity–not with regard to the number of strokes, but to their strength, four or six strokes should be enough for nearly all cases, as the infliction of many but slight strokes in some cases only excite the passions, as Rousseau, in his confessions, tells us.

E. de K. Cambridge.

The last letter to be taken from this paper is one of the most interesting. 'John E.C.H.'s' punishment was to be returned to childhood, which at that time meant wearing skirts, or effectively, girls' clothes. It is a pity that there is no indication as to when this took place.

I have followed with considerable interest the discussion in your columns on 'whipping'. I fail, however, to see why you should describe that time honoured mode of punishment as indecent. Is it indecent for a hospital nurse to wash and otherwise attend to the wants of the patients? Then why should it be thought indecent for a governess to perform certain duties with regard to her pupils? I would ask those who condemn the use of the rod whether children at the present time are more obedient, well-conducted or morally pure than were their fathers and mothers in childhood? Yet it was the rod now quite tabooed, in the fear of which the fathers and mothers were brought up. My advocacy of the judicious use of the rod is based on no mere theoretical grounds. I can speak from experience most personal. Those of your correspondents who have stated or implied that sensuous desires of a certain kind are created by whipping, I assure you that, as far as my recollection goes (and my remembrance on the subject is very vivid), the only effect the rod had on me was the strongest possible intention to avoid in the future the offence which had brought its infliction upon me.

At fourteen years of age I was about as good a specimen of a spoilt child as can

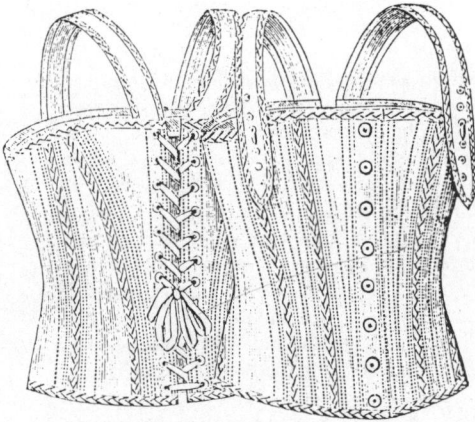

Corset pour petite fille de 8 à 10 ans.
Modèle des *Magasins du Louvre.*

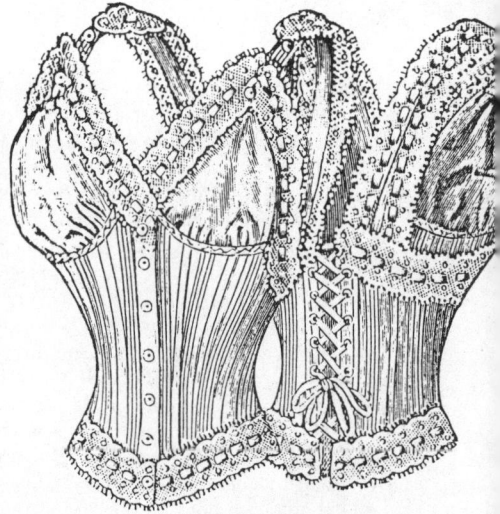

Corset-ceinture pour jeune fille.

Jupons pour fillette.
Modèles des *Magasins du Louvre.*

Jupon en soie.

9. Girl's Underwear.   *La Mode Illustrée*
     Left top – 1894, p. 293.   Right top – 1899, p. 52.
     Left bottom – 1894, p. 50.   Right bottom – 1899, p. 374.

ever be found among the present generation of children. The only son of a wealthy planter, surrounded by slaves, who from infancy had treated me with all the deference due to their future lord, I had grown up ignorant of any will but my own. My father's death placed me under the guardianship of an aunt, who entered me with the least possible delay in a school of some note in Southern Louisiana.

This establishment, conducted by a Spanish lady of good family, consisted besides the school for young and backward boys, of a seminary for ladies, and to this latter was attached an infant class for both boys and girls too young for either of the other two departments. But very few days passed before by disobedience to the governess of my class I had earned the privilege of a private interview with madam. I had already become quite aware of the fact that disobedient children in that establishment were whipped, but even when summoned to madam's room it never entered my mind that anyone would dare, or daring be able, to take such liberty with me. Judge therefore, my astonishment, indignation and fury when, after a very brief struggle with two maid-servants, I found myself stripped to the shirt, fastened face downwards to the sofa. Madam having issued her orders, remained an apparently unconcerned spectator indifferent to my cries; but the use of certain words, which I had been in the habit of applying to offending servants at home, brought upon me the further inconvenience of having a kerchief tied over my mouth. Madam waited till I lay quite exhausted with the vain efforts to free myself, and then with great deliberation began to lecture me on my evil deeds, especially that culminating one, resistance to her chastisement. 'For this, my child, you will receive twenty strokes with this rod.' She placed the long slender bundle of twigs almost under my nose. Again I fought and kicked, but to no purpose. When I had convinced myself of the futility of all resistance, madam proceeded with the same deliberation with the punishment. It need but very few strokes to reduce me to the frame of mind she desired. Not heeding my cries or petitions for mercy she went to the end. Unfastened from the sofa I now knelt before her, and with the greatest readiness obeyed her slightest command. The repetition of a certain formula used on such occasions, acknowledging the fault and thanking madam for the punishment, kissing the rod and finally madam's hand seemed to come quite natural. But a much severer test of that new born obedience followed, when, instead of being allowed to resume my clothes, I was dressed in the costume of a child three or four years old–drawers, petticoats, short dress, all beautifully embroidered and ornamented, and when this toilette was completed I was placed by madam in the Kindergarten class. Of course, it is extremely humiliating for a big boy to be dressed like a little girl, to be made to play with little children, to have to repeat their infantile lessons, to be put to bed at seven o'clock, and, worst of all, to have to submit to a great deal of teasing from the older girls, who delighted in making me carry a doll, and submitting to other indignities; but all aided in producing the one effect desired–prompt obedience to all in authority. When madam considered that lesson had been sufficiently impressed upon me, I was restored to my place in the boys' class and allowed to resume the ordinary dress. I remained a considerable time under madam's charge, but never again incurred punishment for direct disobedience, though like the rest, boys and girls big and little, received punishment for minor offences. This madam, having placed the culprit across her knee, after letting down trousers or drawers, administered with a short rod. Such whipping, though by no means to be incurred lightly, is not to be compared to the birching I have described as my first experience.

Madam's influence over her pupils was unbounded and lasting. I thoroughly believe, were she to confront any of them to-day, grown men or women, those well-remembered words, 'My child, again have you been disobedient; bring me the rod, take off, etc. etc.' would be received with unhesitating obedience, even to assuming the position needed to receive the punishment.   JOHN E.C.H.
Chicago. 1st March

One or two things may be added by way of corroboration. In the first half of the nineteenth century runaway or troublesome slaves in the Southern States of America were occasionally dressed in women's clothes.

A negro fugitive was placed in jail, clad only in a gingham dress, although he was a man. The unusual costume was probably occasioned by the slave's lacerated skin, for even the hardened jailer wrote that he has been lately most inhumanly whipped from his neck down to the feet.[3]

It is not clear whether the explanation for the dress is that given by the newspaper or by the writer, but I suggest that the true reason was more likely to have been to discourage the slave from running away again, or perhaps it was an extra humiliation imposed by his owner before he ran away. Certainly this was the practice of an owner of a plantation situated actually in Louisiana, Bennet H. Barrow, who was born on 21 October 1811. These are entries in his diary:

20 April 1838: Intend making G. Jerry ware womens cloths for running away and without the least cause.

21 July 1839: Gave G. Jerry, Sam Wash and Bartley Bagging skirts to wear–instead of shirt and pants.

24 December 1839: Intend exhibiting Dennis (he had run away) during Christmas on a scaffold in the middle of the Quarter and with a red flannel cap on.

5 July 1840: Negroes appeared quit Lively last night, had the Jack rigged out this evening with red flannel on his years and a Feather in them and sheet on, in the Quarter.

This cotton plantation in the Parish of West Feliciana, east of the Mississippi river, just South of the 31st parallel, must have been not far distant from the school of 'John E. C. H.' in Southern Louisiana. Barrow himself was taught by private tutors until he went to school in Washington, D.C. in 1823.[4]

The letter from 'John E.C.H.' also reminds us to some extent of the incident described in chapter 6 of Mark Twain's *The Adventures of Tom Sawyer* published in 1876. Tom's school is coeducational, with boys on one side of the room and girls on the other. Tom has taken a liking to Becky Thatcher and one morning, on arriving late, he sees that the only vacant seat on the girls' side is next to Becky. When the master asks him why he is late, Tom admits that he has been talking to the notorious urchin Huckleberry Finn. He is told to take his off his jacket and receives a beating. 'Then the order followed: "Now, sir, go and sit with the *girls*! And let this be a warning to you."' Tom goes and sits next to Becky which is the outcome he had hoped to achieve.

Mark Twain (Samuel Langhorne Clemens) was born in Florida, Missouri in 1835 and went to school there until about 1850. His experience of school life may be nearly contemporary with that of 'John E.C.H.' The episode suggests that sitting with the girls was one of the punishments imposed at that time, when boys and girls were taught in the same room but on separate sides of it. Presumably Tom remained without his jacket as he sat next to Becky. But what did the schoolmaster mean by his warning? Was there the possibility of a girl's pinafore or some other article of girl's attire for the unfortunate boy? This idea was in fact taken up by another American writer, Irvin Shrewsbury Cobb (1876-1944), who was born in Paducah in the neighbouring state of Kentucky. He also wrote about a boy hero who gets into scrapes, John C. Calhoun Custer, Junior, under the title, *Goin' On Fourteen*. Although this was published in 1924, the time of the story is the previous century, in the middle of the Fauntleroy craze of the late eighteen eighties. In chapter XX, 'Little short Pantsleroy', Junior excites giggles and whispers when he arrives in the Friday afternoon class dressed in his hated new Fauntleroy suit. On the way he has been jeered at by his enemy, Lish Riley, who threatens to beat him up on his way home.

'I want a little quiet,' Miss Ida would demand. 'How can you expect somebody to recite a nice interesting piece when you boys keep on giggling and whispering among yourselves every time my back is turned. I warrant you the first thing you all know somebody is going to regret misbehaving. I won't have such goings-on, you hear me! You know what I'll do, too. The very next sound I hear out of one of you boys I'm going to do exactly what I did only here just the other day to Waller Wilcox, sitting yonder.'

In the next chapter, 'Brer Rabbit, He Lay Low', we learn what was done to Waller Wilcox 'the other day'. He was made to wear a girl's bonnet. Needless to say Junior, because he is so distracted by the costume he is wearing, lets out a rude remark which is reported to the teacher. He is ordered up to the platform.

For a long half-minute she visited her silent wrath upon him. She had decided what punishment this high crime merited; only a little while before she had given intimation that she might revive it. It was a form of degradation devised by her some days earlier for treating with flagrant masculine offenders. But before she invoked it she would abash and devastate him with her eyes. She did so, to the full. Then, without turning her look from the sagged object of it, she made a request out of a corner of her compressed lips.

'Milly Hollander,' she said, 'will you please lend me your sunbonnet? Order there!' she snapped, stilling the gleeful anticipatory titter and gurgle which, at this, ran through the ranked desks. 'This is no laughing matter.'

Right gladly Milly Hollander hurried to a line of hooks set in the back wall of the room and brought her sunbonnet to her teacher. It was a blue sunbonnet, fluted and ribbed and flouncy, and of a pattern which almost has vanished from some parts since the race learned that complexions no longer need these artificial shadings to preserve them from sunburn and the winds that tan a tender skin, inasmuch as better ones may be had in handy packages of the nearest druggist or department store. It was a veritable funnel and scoop-shovel of a sunbonnet, with skirts on it to shroud the owner's neck at the back and with broad strings to be tied in at the throat.

In the midst of a joyous hush Miss Ida Brazell fitted this cavernous adornment upon the offender's bowed head and made its starchy cambric ribands fast beneath his swallowed-up chin and smoothed its abundant draperies out upon his drooping shoulders.

'Now then, she said, 'you'll wear that until school is dismissed. And if I hear another word from you–if you so much as whisper–I don't know what I'll do to you! But it will be something you won't forget in a hurry–even if I have to put a girl's dress on you instead of just a girl's bonnet. Go back to your seat and stay there!'

Junior defies Miss Brazell because he has a plan inspired by the story of the Tar-Baby hinted at in the title of the chapter.[5] He therefore deliberately courts the punishment threatened, which he sees will save him from both Lish Riley and his mother.

'So you dare me, do you?' she sputtered. 'You take me at my word and dare me to do it, do you? Well, we'll see about that, right this minute.' She left off shaking him to send an inquiring eye roving over the scrooging expectant assemblage, then brought it back again and focussed it on a quivering individual in the immediate foreground.

'Clara Belle,' she said, 'wonder if you wouldn't let me have that nice pretty big white apron you're wearing, for a little while?'

'Oh, yessum, Miss Ida.' The informer gasped in her delight. With a nimble twist she was up and out in the aisle. Clara Belle might never be able to throw a baseball or a stone, save with an awkward overhand heave but, since nature balances all things, she could do what none of the opposite sex could do; she could reach up between her own shoulder-blades and instantly overcome the intricacies of a garment fastening in the back.

On this occasion she probably broke her own best previous record. Her fingers made flickering play like lightning with all the buttons and all the button-holes–and of these there were many, extending all the way down her rear latitudes from hem to hem. For Clara Belle's starchiest apron fulfilled an utilitarian as well as an ornamental purpose. Its broad crisp sash, encircling her high under the armpits, its puffy sleeves, its tucked and ruffled yoke with rick-rack embroidery on it–these were brilliantly decorative, it is true, but by its length it gave Clara Belle protection from chalk-dust and street-dust.

'Hold out your arms, John Custer,' commanded Miss Ida Brazell, when Clara Belle had unenveloped her eager self. Under this final crushing stroke his spirit apparently had broken. Almost with a seeming willingness he did as bidden. 'Now, turn round.'

He turned round.

Painstakingly and omitting no button, she buttoned him up. She tied the sash, cruelly elaborating the design of its bow. She stood off and contemplated her handiwork, the onlookers muffling their gorgeous emotions as best they might, but not succeeding by any means.

'I'm sorry for you,' said Miss Ida, 'that there has to be a boy like you in the Fifth grade. I'm sorry for myself that I have to have a boy like you in my grade. I'm sorry for all the rest of my scholars that they have to mix with a boy like you. Now go and stand up there right alongside my table so everybody can have a good look at you. I'll show you whether you can run rough-shod over this whole school.'

But Junior simply walks right out of the class and straight past Lish Riley who thinks he is a girl. At home he tells his mother that the teacher made him wear the girl's clothes because she was sorry for him and he preferred to leave them on going home rather than be seen in the Fauntleroy suit. His mother relents and Junior gives the suit to a black boy. The writer cleverly emphasises the extreme femininity of the garments, the way the teacher relishes her task of dressing a boy as a girl and the delight of the audience, especially the girls, in seeing this being done.

This series of the paper came to an end on 28 November 1885. I do not know why. Perhaps Rosenberg went to prison again. A third and final series ran from 1 October 1887 to 21 July 1888.[6]

1   James Brough, *The Prince and the Lily* (London: Hodder & Stoughton, 1975), chapters 8 and 9.

2   'E.' obviously intended, but there had been a letter signed 'E.I.' in the issue for 19 May, a letter which had also been lifted from the *E.D.M.* April 1870 Supplement.

3   Charles Sackett Sydnor, *Slavery in Mississippi* (New York: American Historical Association, 1933), p. 90, quoting *The Woodville Republican*, 11 September 1830.

4   *Plantation Life in the Florida Parishes of Louisiana 1836-46, as reflected in the Diary of Bennet H. Barrow*, edited by Edwin Adams Davis, (New York: Columbia Univerity Press, 1943).

5   Joel Chandler Harris (1848-1908), *Uncle Remus* (1880), chs. 2 and 4.

6   *Town Talk* has another claim to fame. From 12 May 1883 to 28 June 1884 it printed a translation of Zola's *Nana* (1880). This must be the translation by Henry Vizitelly which he published in book form in 1884, and for which he was later prosecuted. See Graham King, *Garden of Zola* (London: Barrie and Jenkins, 1978), although King does not seem to know of the serialisation in *Town Talk*.

V

THE FAMILY DOCTOR AND PEOPLE'S MEDICAL ADVISER

On 21 February 1885 *Town Talk* announced: 'The publisher of that interesting journal the "Police News" is about to issue a paper called the "Family Doctor and People's Medical Adviser." The Journal will be devoted to the cure of all forms of disease.' Rosenberg then added the suggestion that undertakers should advertise in it. By the 'Police News' he meant *The Illustrated Police News* (1867 to 1938). The paper duly came out on 7 March 1885 published by George Purkess of 286, Strand.

How far the paper fulfilled its task with sound medical advice, I am not qualified to say. It did, however, publish articles setting out the dangers of tight lacing and wearing high-heeled boots and shoes. Three major articles with illustrations showing the results of tight lacing were printed on 2 February, 6 March and 20 March 1886. Some of the pages of these articles have been torn or cut out of the volumes in the British Newspaper Library. Immediately men and women wrote in supporting or disagreeing with the articles, the first, 'A Victim to Fashion,' on 27 March 1886 obviously in agreement. 'Lover of Stays,' however, a man, on 22 May 1886, disagreed. From then onwards until 1894 the paper published hundreds of letters on all aspects of the corset and high heel, not to mention corporal punishment in all its varieties, gloves, earrings and spurs for ladies. In short all of and more than the subjects covered in the 'Englishwoman's Conversazione.' In particular in this periodical male cross dressing was openly discussed in the press for the first time. All such letters I have included in my *Men in Petticoats*. I am now selecting letters which deal with boys wearing stays or some article of female clothing either as ordinary wear or for moral improvement.

Sometimes this was for reasons of health. 'An Old Stay-Wearer and Tight Lacer' wrote on 12 June 1886: 'A delicate, ailing lad, almost always in the doctor's hands, my mother, to give me increased support and to improve my health, put me at twelve or fourteen years of age into good, stout, well-fitting, and full boned stays. My health at once improved, and for the last thirty years has been thoroughly good.' Philip Willing, however, apparently born in 1842, suffered much from early stay-wearing.

TIGHT LACING   11 December 1886, p. 231.
The adherents of tight-lacing and figure forming have had a good deal of their own way lately, and proved, or tried to prove, how little they have suffered from continued encasement in a corset. As I have not come through the ordeal so satisfactorily, it may be that my experience will be a slight change from the monotony of success. As a boy of five I was sent to reside with an aunt of mine who was, unfortunately, inbred with the idea that her duty to posterity was to start them on life's course with perfect figures. To this end her daughters–my cousins–were wearing the smallest of corsets and being educated under the old ridiculous regime of reclining boards, stocks and back-boards. At seven I too came in for a share of the physical improvement, and despite severe struggles, I was duly measured and enclosed in a hard, unstretchable little corset that held in my poor little body, and made my till then merry existence a dreary round of erect postures and stiffened movements. Regularly I would cut my laces or break short the bones of my corset, until I was as regularly stuck in the corner with my poor little fists thrust into a sort of muff, the two ends of which were strapped round my wrists. This preliminary training I endured till the age of ten, when I believe I really liked to

FASHIONS FOR THE SEASON.

357

The Ladies' Treasury, 1858, I, 337.

10. Fashions for the Season.

be tightly laced, and I know that my will had so far succumbed to that of my aunt that I meekly had my toes turned outwards for three or four hours a day in the 'stocks,' while my elbows and shoulders were forced back by the wretched torture of the back-board. From ten to fifteen I know I took considerable pride in the cultivation of my waist, which was then in a tightly-laced condition that allowed it only to measure some fifteen inches. I attended dancing classes and went to parties, and became so generally forced into juvenile feminine society that my ideas were limited to the extent of half-hearted robustness that I saw around me. A few months from my fifteenth birthday the first symptoms of spinal curvature presented themselves, and under medical advice my stays were removed. But then the injury was done. My back, weakened by a long and severe (as I now think) course of tight lacing, was too infirm to remain erect when its false supports were removed, and the curve became more and more pronounced. I went back to my corset, but after four months of freedom I found I could not bear its confinement. Then I had to lie down, and for three weary years I was confined to a couch, whereon I lay perfectly flat, with little more than a dull ceiling to rest my gaze upon. At nineteen I rose much weakened, but, as I thought, cured, and for a change of scene set out for a south coast village, where I spent a most happy season of con-valescence. But even then the effects of my early training were not to leave me, for within a year it became necessary for me to seek medical treatment, for again the cur-vature appeared. This time I would not lie down for a further time of misery, so after a consultation of deep import I came to London and was fitted with a spinal appliance that embraced the trunk, and during the time of wearing at least made my body as straight as in its earliest years. At night I wore a sort of corset to maintain the position enforced by the appliance during the day, and during five years I endured the trouble of changing twice daily from one to the other, and the fatigue of wearing upon my body a mass of steel and leather, through the gross infatuation of an aunt who would endeavour to make my appearance better than God thought fit to ordain. Since then I have been immovably 'set' in plaster, and undergone all sorts of treatment from the gymnastic to the poro-plastic, but here I am, at forty-four, barely able to walk two miles, and suffering daily humiliation at the hands of my valet, who will shortly enter to know if I am pleased to be helped off my couch and secured with five straps into the appliance, by whose aid alone I am able to keep my chest and knees from meeting. Hang tight-lacing Mr. Editor! I say. Hoping for an era when our girls will have more sense than to run the risk of becoming semi-helpless cripples.   PHILIP WILLING

When boys and girls were brought up together and the girls were strictly corseted, the same treatment was sometimes applied to the boys. 'Beautiful Bride' of Highgate (25 December 1886, p. 263), four sisters and a brother were brought up in Paris by an aunt who was extremely particular about their appearance. Special attention was paid to the girls' hands. 'Our figures were also cultivated to an extraordinary degree. My brother was always made to wear a stiff, very tight corset, but unlike your correspondent, Mr. Willing, he has never suffered from it, perhaps because he was not put into stays till he was fourteen, and gradually accustomed to be laced tighter and tighter; also, his stays were so low as to allow the development of his chest.' I quote the whole of the next letter as the brother's figure training followed that of his sister.

1 January 1887, p. 279.
Having read with much interest the recent correspondence on stays and tight lac-ing, I should like to give you my experiences. My mother was a great believer in the benefits of corsets, and as children my brother and myself both wore them; so unlike most boys, he was accustomed to the restraint, and did not mind it. When I was four-teen I was measured for my first real stays, and on their arrival put into a strict course

of lacing. These stays were very stiff and strongly boned, with a broad busk and side steels, and would not give or stretch in the least. The first day I was laced in from twenty-five to twenty inches, which made the stays fit quite tight, and caused me to grumble a good deal, as I could not bend or stoop, but I soon got used to this, and did not mind it. I was then tightened in every day a little till my waist was only eighteen inches. This I felt very irksome, and often wished to loosen them, as it quite took my breath away; but my mother would not allow this, so I had to keep quiet and make the best of it.

A corset was also made for me to sleep in; it was rather looser, but quite as stiff as the one I wore during the day, and was fastened so that I could not take it off.

The next proceeding was to make me perfectly upright by means of shoulder braces. These were fastened to the stays, and being drawn tightly behind, my shoulders were forced back and held so firmly that it was impossible to stoop or even reach forward.

No further alteration was made in the size of my waist for nearly a year, at the end of which time, when about fifteen, I was laced in at night to seventeen inches, and a new corset made with a waist of only fifteen inches, and between the corset-maker and my own maid I was laced into it. In a short time it began to hurt a good deal, and I could not help crying when my mother forbade me to be loosened till bedtime; but after a few days I found she was right, as it ceased to hurt and made my figure look awfully nice. Of course, I could not run or make any exertion, but as the training I had been accustomed to had always prevented this, I was quite happy without. In the meantime my brother's figure had also received due attention. When he was fourteen he was put into a stiff pair of stays, which were gradually tightened till his waist was as small and trim as a girl's. He was kept in these for some months till he was accustomed to the compression. He was then made to wear them at night and a new pair made for ordinary wear. These measured nineteen inches round the waist and were much more stiffly boned. When they were laced up he was as tightly encased as myself, the stiff steel busk in the corsets and a pair of strong shoulder braces, which were strapped as tightly as possible, quite preventing him from stooping. Before going to a party we were both even more strictly treated, my brother's stays having a waist of eighteen inches and my own only thirteen and a half. I have to put these on some time before dressing, lacing them tighter by degrees. The sensation of wearing these stays is most delightful, although they are so tight I can hardly breathe when they are first laced close. I always dance better in them, and sometimes wear them during the day. I have also been accustomed to wear the tightest high-heeled boots possible, and can walk quite well in them. My hands too, have been taken great care of. Since I was about thirteen I have worn gloves day and night; those worn during the day have always been so tight that I could hardly use my hands, which are consequently very small and beautifully white from being constantly covered.

In the above description of our figure training, I have forgotten to mention that our diet was strictly regulated, as we were never allowed anything fattening, and, after each meal, at least an hour was spent on a reclining board. As children, we were punished by being laced tighter than usual–the stays not being loosened again for perhaps a week.

Notwithstanding this treatment, we both enjoy very good health, and have not the slightest intention of leaving off corsets. My waist, now I am nineteen years old, is fourteen inches, and with very little trouble I can lace myself an inch smaller. I generally sleep in stays, letting them out about an inch.

My brother's waist is nineteen inches, and he wears his stays day and night without loosening them, intending shortly to reduce his waist to eighteen inches. He likes to be laced in as tightly as possible, and on one occasion, when trying on a pair of my stays, he laced them by degrees till his waist was only sixteen inches, and wore them for over an hour. Apologising for the length of this letter.

Kensington, Dec. 17th.   A GIRL WITH A TIGHT WAIST

On 26 June 1886 'A Hater of Humbug,' apparently born about 1836, had contributed a letter defending the wearing of stays by men. In a later letter he gave further details of his childhood.

9 June 1888, p. 234.

I was a fair-haired boy, with a sister just a year older than myself, and we were remarkably alike; and my mother for a long time liked to dress us alike in many respects. My hair was kept long, parted down the middle and dressed exactly as my sister's; my underclothing was like hers, including the stays; and we both wore side-laced boots, that in those days were worn by girls and ladies; the only difference between us was that I wore a blouse and short trousers and my sister a petticoat and frock. When, at fourteen, I was sent to one of the large public schools, my hair was cut short, my stays were left at home, and boys' boots were procured for me. I developed a decided aptitude for athletics, and excelled in all of them–cricket, football, rackets, rowing, etc., etc. When I came home for the holidays, by my mother's wish I resumed my stays, and the wearing of ladies' boots and gloves, as my hands and feet are small.

London, May 10th.   A HATER OF HUMBUG

The writer went on to say that he still wore stays and, to please his wife, ladies' boots. 'H.W.' was a schoolmaster whose wife helped him with his pupils. Letters about her beautiful hands and the punishments she had inflicted on boys by slapping their faces with her gloved hand or by caning their gloved hands appeared on 12 May, 9 June and 14 July 1888. On his letter of 9 June, 'A Sister to Six Brothers' made this comment: 'how a boy of seventeen years can stand being sent for in the drawing-room simply to have his ears boxed, by a girl two years his senior, "at least a dozen times," I cannot understand–he must be a duffer'. 'Eperon', however, claimed that he had suffered something similar at a school run by ladies. For drill he had also had to wear stays, boots and gloves. This is the first correspondent to allege such treatment in an English school.

CORPORAL PUNISHMENT IN SCHOOLS   28 July 1888, p. 345.

I was much interested in the letter in the last number from 'H.W.', which was particularly interesting to me, as I myself had some few years ago a prolonged opportunity of tasting both the punishments described. Certainly, I can emphatically confirm from sharp experience his statement that the pain given by the whip cutting is 'very severe,' indeed the expression errs on the side of mildness.

Until between fifteen and sixteen I was at ordinary schools, but was then removed to one kept by an elderly lady, who was assisted by three governesses and her own daughter, a very pretty girl, dressed always in the height of fashion, who had herself not long left a very strict finishing school. The discipline was very strict, and I was surprised to find how quickly I, though not reported at my former schools more mild than the rest of the world, fell in with the rules. We were never allowed to indulge in the boisterous shouting common in boys' schools, nor to talk in the bedrooms or passages. Ordinarily we were dressed like other youths, but Mondays, Wednesdays, and Fridays were 'smart days', on which we had a turn of dancing or drilling. On these days we wore a dress consisting of smooth drab cloth knickerbockers and tunic, fitting closely over a very tightly-laced, long-waisted, fashionable corset, and having short-wristed sleeves, under which passed the upper part of long tight kid gloves. The boots were of black kid, laced high in the ankles, extremely tight and pointed, and with very high heels. Woe betide the unlucky wight who danced a false step or made a false turn at drill. Although immediately upon leaving this school, which was not until I was over eighteen, I cast away stays, long gloves, and ladies' boots, I must confess that I never suffered any harm from their use. And unpleasant as was the frequent punishment, I must admit that I have never known a better conducted school, or one where better progress was made.

I should like to know whether Mrs. H.W., as our pretty tyrant used to do, makes her pupils kiss the tips of her gloved hand after receiving the punishment. To have to do this gracefully, in view of the laughing smile of the fair punisher, is not the least part of the punishment. It would be very interesting if Mrs. H.W. would tell us how long she has held sway at her husband's school, and what difference her method has made, and how it was received at first.

With regard to the ladies' dress controversy, allow me to say that, notwithstanding all the marble Venuses in the world, I ardently admire a long, slender waist, and consider that a pretty hand never looks so pretty as when encased in a many buttoned light kid glove as tight as possible, that a pretty boot should be high-heeled and narrow-toed, and that a tight glove-like fit is infinitely nice. –Yours truly,   EPERON

P.S. By the way, from H.W.'s manner of mentioning the riding whip I infer that his wife rides. Does she use a spur? The young lady to whose tender care we were chiefly indebted for the stinging slaps and the sharp cuts upon our hands, and on 'smart days,' upon our stockings and thin kid boots also, was a great rider, and her fiery steed was always noticeable, as riding upon the curb, she made him prance and caper.

This may be the same 'Eperon' who wrote about the use of the spur by ladies in the *The Englishwoman's Domestic Magazine* for March 1869. He contributed a letter on high heels on 20 April 1889. The next correspondent describes a situation where stays, boots, and gloves are imposed not at a school but by a stepmother. This is the first of many such.

TIGHT LACING   18 August 1888, p. 391.
I wish a 'Sister of Six Brothers' would give me a receipt for emancipation from female rule. I am a lad seventeen years old, and am compelled by my stepmother, who is five years older, to always attend her, to lace up her boots, button her gloves, etc., and I am now being taught to do her hair. She makes me wear stays laced in to nineteen inches (I am five feet four inches in height), knickerbockers, and silk stockings, with very high-heeled boots buttoned high up the leg, and six-button gloves, and I well know the weight of her small soft hands and very often the force of her pretty little foot. Yours truly,   W.S.   Westbourne Terrace, W. 14th July.

F. Paget, however, yielded to gentle persuasion, but not his brother.

TIGHT LACING AND HIGH HEELS   6 October 1888, p. 87.
The correspondence on 'Tight Lacing and High Heels' seems to go on unabated. Will you allow me to give, as one of the male sex, my personal experience? Some months ago I and my younger brother went to live with a maiden aunt. She has been trying for a considerable time to get me to adopt the wearing of corsets, and I laughed at the idea, until, going to live with her, she persuaded me to try them. She introduced me to a fashionable corsetiere, who made me a pair to order, and I, being tall and slim, laced into twenty-three inches without much inconvenience, and have since gradually reduced myself, with the assistance of the housemaid, who laces me, about a quarter of an inch each week, until now I have laced comfortably into nineteen inches. I have just had a lovely pair of corsets made, exactly as a lady's, fitted on, covered with mauve satin, and elaborately trimmed, seventeen inches in the waist, though I shall only lace

in at the starting to nineteen inches. So far as experience goes, at first the feeling was decidedly unique, and not altogether pleasant, but now on getting accustomed to it, I rather like it than otherwise, and don't think I have deteriorated in health by it. I see some of my companions drink and smoke immoderately–both of which I do very moderately–with far more injury to their health than I imagine tight lacing would do.

My aunt has been trying to coax my young brother, aged twelve, to wear corsets, high heels, and long gloves; but without success, so that she is anxious to place him under the control of a lady governess at a school similar to those mentioned by several of your correspondents, if any of them would kindly send address to the undermentioned address. F. PAGET.   2A Somerset-terrace, High-street, Kensington, Sept. 21st 1888.

This is another accomodation address. According to *Kelly's Directory* of 1892 the occupiers of 2A, Somerset-terrace were James Frederick Lincoln Jeffery, tobacconist and Mrs. Emily Bren, confectioner. 'K.' also wanted to know about schools, making the following request in the 'Notes and Queries' column of 15 December 1888: 'I should be much obliged if you would ask in the next number of the FAMILY DOCTOR if any of your correspondents would send me the address of a school where girls have their figures thoroughly trained; and also if one is known where boys can be treated in the same way?' She received this reply from 'F.M.' on 29 December 1888 (p. 283): '"K." will find it difficult to meet with a suitable school. There is one in Maida Vale, W. and several, I believe, at Brighton; no boys' schools of that sort exist here, though in Paris and Vienna they could be found. "K." would do far better to train their figures herself; I speak from experience, having successfully done so to three daughters and advised a lady friend about her son of thirteen.' The next correspondent fully expounded the theory of corset discipline in schools and claimed that such schools existed.

AUSTRIAN DISCIPLINE SCHOOLS   18 May 1889, p. 184.
I have long thought that what is called 'Figure-Training' may be utilised in a direction little known in this country, though perfectly understood in France and Austria. Recent facts which have come to my knowledge have confirmed this view, and shown me that the most potent of all known methods of dealing with the 'bumptiousness' of modern youth is absolutely neglected here through ignorance of its practical value. At the same time, no doubt the virulence of the self-styled 'Hygienic' party is still an obstacle so great as almost to preclude parents and guardians from assisting their other efforts for the good of their children by the utilisation of the corset.

The correspondence in your journal has conclusively shown that (under proper supervision, and in the hands of reasonable people) no harm of a physical nature results: whilst great moral improvement undoubtedly follows when a proper system of mental training is connected therewith. Of course it is not contended that well-behaved children need, or would be benefited by any kind of special discipline, but the class that does need it is daily increasing, and ought to be considered as requiring as distinct a method of education from ordinary children as those who amongst the poorer classes are confined in what are called 'reformatories.' The benefits, however, of the latter institutions are restricted exclusively to the poor, whilst the children of the upper classes often stand quite as much in need of special supervision as any that are placed therein. Under these circumstances a few schools have been established in England for special discipline, but so little are they in harmony with the modern notion that parents are to give way to children on all points, that they dare not even publish their addresses, and up to the present time I am actually unacquainted with a single proprietor, although I know of some localities where schools exist, in which the corset-discipline is practised. When we speak of discipline we must remember that tightness is a question of measurement and degree, and that what one understands by the term is different from that intended by another. But I believe the schools in question advocate and maintain the use of an actual amount of uncomfortable pressure as a means of restraint, and as an evidence of submission, as well as an excellent means of improving the carriage and promoting elegance of appearance. It is quite natural that those who know nothing of the beneficial results thus produced, should regard this as a mere 'fad,' or possibly as an anachronism, deserving of the severest condemnation.

At first sight it must appear unaccountable that moral good could be obtained by eccentricity of costume or restriction of what are, in ordinary cases, justly regarded as wholesome activities. But on further enquiry I find that the method pursued has some advantages, not only for girls, but also for boys who have evinced an overbearing and intractable disposition. For it is found that the restriction above-mentioned renders it easier for ladies to take the government into their own hands without the assistance of masters, and as they alone can carry out a system of domestic supervision in all its details, this gives the schools in question an advantage otherwise absolutely unobtainable.

Of course the mere wearing of stays (however sedative, both from a mental and physical point of view) is only one element of the system pursued, but it is properly made the basis of all, as without it the other details would insensibly be got rid of, and the school revert to the ordinary type.

It would be too much to expect that the conventional pedagogue should look upon such a method of moral training without hatred and contempt. He despises that which he does not understand,and declaims about the primary necessity of making boys 'manly.' True manliness is good if it can be combined with other good qualities, but practically we often find that it is this premature notion of being 'manly' before the proper time, that is at the bottom of half the misconduct of children who are running in the broadway that leadeth to destruction. When the notion is further encouraged by foolish mothers and selfish so-called 'friends of the family,' a condition of awful depravity is often established, where different circumstances would have produced opposite results.

When the proper time comes, in the judgement of the boys' natural guardians, then a totally different physical method ought, in some cases, to be pursued, but not until obedience, respectfulness, and a habit of deferring to the judgement of older persons is fully established. In this way boys get the right kind of start in life, and are in almost every respect, better situated as regards their own future, whilst the homes which their misconduct has disgraced and degraded may become again examples of punctuality, politeness, and orderly Christian behaviour. I am, etc.

MEDICUS PARENS   London, 6 April 1889.

Three weeks later the paper printed a long letter from 'Admirer of Pretty Feet' supporting the arguments of 'Medicus Parens', and giving his experience of the discipline they both recommended. This writer does not mention the other, so presumably it was composed before he had seen the issue of May 18.

DISCIPLINE   8 June 1889, pp. 232-3.

The present tendency to luxury renders good discipline daily of more and more importance, and youths are in the nature of things even more liable to injury from unbridled license than are girls. For them, therefore, even more than for their sisters, a period of discipline is extremely valuable; and in the course of discipline both direct punishment and a certain amount of general curbing and restraint are most desirable. In this connection the compulsory wearing of stays at once suggests itself as equally beneficial to either sex. Of course, by stays I do not mean the absurd flimsy things one only too often notices, but good, strongly-boned, stiff-busked, firm corsets, producing an elegant, long-waisted, tapering figure, and rendering impossible all indulgence in unseemly careless lolling about. The corset is the very type of good discipline, and to be thoroughly well corseted without reference to whether he will or no, is an excellent reminder to any lad, no matter how much impressed with his own importance, that he cannot have all his own way. The degree of tightness must vary, of course, in particular cases, but as a general rule it may be considered that in a moderate time any pupil, whether youth or girl, may be required to lace to two-thirds of the natural waist measures. Strict uniformity of lacing should, however, be avoided, every pupil having a corset for ordinary wear, and one for best an inch tighter and extra stiff. At least two days in the week there should be some active exercise without the corset, as by this means the natural figure is preserved and the effect of the corset made much more beneficial both as regards discipline and as regards appearance. Of course, however, the details of when relaxation is to be allowed and when extra restraint is to be applied, must be left to the unquestioned discretion of the powers that be.

I can quite well fancy some horrible screaming by some of the sentimental amongst your readers at the idea of compulsory 'tight-lacing'; but it is the necessary sacrifice of a certain degree of ease and comfort, which is its special merit so far as discipline is concerned, and for which it is deliberately chosen. In the same way use may be made of long kid gloves of delicate tints, which are required to be kept fresh and unsoiled; and so also with thin kid boots with very high heels tapering to an extremely small base. Both gloves and boots should, of course, be the very tightest fit. It is wonderful how neat the feet and hands can thus be made to appear, and I cannot blame a lady for smartening up her charges in this way, even if it were only for her preference as a matter of dressiness to having them about her in freedom, roughness, and all the glory of independent rudeness. Many Austrian ladies, indeed, do have pages of gentle birth, whom they take solely for the gratification of their own vanity in having such smart attendants, and with whom they are extremely strict; the pages being thus put out by their friends on purpose to have the benefit of the discipline; which if the lady happens to be quick tempered, is at times very sharp indeed, as I have the best of reasons to recollect, having for two years been in attendance upon an extremely pretty girl of about three and twenty, a most capricious martinet.

As to the best persons to administer discipline, I have not a moment's hesitation in giving my voice in favour of the fair sex. It is quite a different thing for a lad to cower under the bullying of some burly pedagogue, and for him to be sharply disciplined by one whose reliance is not upon physical strength, but upon the privilege of her sex. In the one case it is a mere keeping down by sheer might; in the other the pupil is learning to yield and bend his will not to power but to duty.

I know it is often said, as if it were something very wonderful indeed, that a young lady set in authority over pupils of the opposite sex, perhaps only a few years her juniors, and knowing herself free from the possibility of retaliation, is apt to become tyrannical. It is quite true, and the discipline is so much the better so far as the pupils are concerned, so they have no cause to complain. With regard to the lady, it should be remembered that it is one of the privileges of a pretty woman to be tyrannical: and I do not see why a pretty woman should not avail herself of her privileges just as well as anyone else.

From fifteen to sixteen and a half I was at a very strict discipline school. Thence I passed under the gentle dominion of the young lady I have already mentioned. I dare say if there had been anyone to tell me I was cruelly used I should have been thoroughly miserable, but as there was not I was perfectly happy, and not a little vain of the elegant appearance I made in the smart dresses I was required to wear [he means, I think, smart male costumes]. I do not pretend that I liked pain any better than other people, though I had extremely good opportunities of judging what a small hand

59

can do, either in the way of administering ringing slaps upon one's cheeks, or applying a riding whip in any available place, whether hands or feet, or arms or legs, and can pronounce silk tights to be a most insufficient protection against a jockey's whip handled by an angry woman. But the prettiness and piquant *soupcon* of vanity of my young patroness rendered it impossible to bear malice towards her even when most exacting. So I was perfectly happy, and I am perfectly certain that the sharp discipline I underwent did me an immense deal of good.

May I just say another word or two in answer to some questions that have appeared in your paper?

First as to the odious habit of biting the nails. This is most disgusting in either sex, and must be stopped however severe the means that have to be employed. I remember a young lady, who after numerous devices had been tried in vain, was at length cured by being made to wear gloves with needles sewn into the finger tips. To prevent her taking these off she had metal bracelets, which tightly clasped her wrists and fastened with springs that could only be undone with a key which was kept by her maid.

I have seen a similar device applied to the ankles of a young lady who insisted upon taking off in the house the very tight boots which her mother required her to wear.

The best cure for anyone who will unlace a corset is to take a little piece of strong, thin chain and fasten it just loosely round the corset waist with a little padlock. There is no discomfort, and the pupil, so long as he or she submits, need not even know the guard is on, so far as feeling it goes. But let the adventurous spirit cut the lace, and a very different tale is told. I have never known anyone repeat the experiment. I tried it once in early days, and found that quite enough. I cut the lace in the afternoon, and I shall never forget the tender weal I wore for days after, for the key was not brought to my assistance until bedtime.

To cure a habit of stooping whilst sitting, there should be an extra stiff busk, a good deal curved in at the bottom, inserted after the corset is laced on. If the head is persistently stooped also, a wooden ball may be fastened under the chin, having a darning needle fixed in its centre. Before I was taken in hand I stooped and slouched in a way that made my stepmother almost ashamed to let me walk with her, and I can vouch for the method of cure I have described being most efficacious.–I am, Sir, your obedient servant,　　　　　　　　　　　　　　　　　　　**ADMIRER OF PRETTY FEET**

The following correspondent supported the idea of corset discipline having worn corsets himself for medical reasons.

CORSET DISCIPLINE　　　　　　　　　　　　　　　　　　29 June 1889, p. 281.

Being very much interested in the correspondence that has been going on in your valuable paper for the past few weeks, I should like to write a few lines on the subject of corset discipline . I am a married man of eleven years' standing, with two children, and my age is thirty-five years. I write from experience I have gained, not only in this country, but abroad, and from what I have heard from those who are in a position to give an opinion on the subject.

Some years ago I suffered much from spinal weakness and indigestion, also at times from giddiness, and was then advised to try if the wearing of properly-made, slightly-laced stays would do my general health good. At that time I measured some 30 inches round waist, chest 35, and hips 34, my height being 5 feet 7 inches; but after following my friend's advice and wearing a well-made perfect-fitting lady's corset, waist measure 25 inches, I was gradually reduced to that size, and my measurements are now–waist 25 inches, chest 36½ inches, and hips 35 inches. I am also slightly taller, as I do not now stoop, being supported and strengthened by the firm grasp of my corsets. I could easily wear a corset of 23 inches waist measurement without any discomfort, but there is no need for me to do so, as I do not wear this article of dress for appearance, but for comfort and my health's sake. I at first wore my corsets both during night and day so as to give the treatment as fair a trial as possible, and soon found great benefit from their constant use. As I gradually laced my waist, small by degrees and beautifully less, so my general health and strength improved.

My business leads me to be more or less active, and some days I walk from ten to fifteen miles without feeling done up, like many young men whom one meets in the present day, who think it wonderful to walk three or four miles of a Saturday afternoon. I am also fond of rowing, and bathe much when at seaside, so you will see that my corsets, though tightly laced, do not prevent my taking healthy exercise, but rather tend to assist me in doing so.

Ladies and gentlemen, girls and boys, would, I am sure, derive great benefit by the judicious use of the corset, and were it more used for both sexes I doubt if there would be so much bodily suffering as there is at present.

Being tightly laced acts as a good disciplinarian, and prevents over-indulgence in both eating and drinking, which is the cause of so many of the ills that man is heir to. I think corset training at schools should be brought more into use both for girls and boys. Those who were difficult to manage and careless about their carriage could be put under a strict course of figure training; but due regard must be had to health in using this restraint. To be extra tightly laced would serve as a great punishment in cases of misconduct, and would prevent the pupil from taking part for the time being (at least, with any comfort) in the usual games and amusements. If stooping (which is one of the great causes of indigestion) is indulged in the pupil might with great advantage be obliged to wear a back board or extra long busk during school hours.

This discipline would make the girl or boy subjected to it more tractable to the ladies having their management, as they could always threaten them if disobedient with a tightening of their already tight corsets to the extent of an inch or more for long or short periods. This threat would be quite sufficient, and they would feel that they were not their own masters in everything, and learn to bend their will to those placed over them. I think this system, if not carried to a ridiculous extreme, a more reasonable way of guiding the young than that ancient and barbarous custom advocated by so many of those who have written to your paper–I mean birching and flogging. I should make it very disagreeable for any master or mistress at any school who would punish my boy or girl in such a way. I am, however, happy to say that they do not require any severe measures being used, and my wife and I find that a kind word and a little reasoning is all that is required when they are disobedient.

The corset system of training has no danger under the care of a judicious and experienced lady, and who but a lady can give that gentle polish to the manner and bearing of both girls and boys?–I am, dear Sir, yours faithfully,

EXPERIMENTUM CRUCIS

P.S. Shall be glad to privately give any information I can to your readers.

London, June 13 1889.

The very next letter in the paper is from someone who has had personal experience of corset discipline.

29 June 1889, pp. 281-2.

Your correspondent who wrote on the subject of discipline in your number for the 8th of June ['Admirer of Pretty Feet'] gives some most useful hints as to the beneficial results of corset-wearing as a restraining and curbing correction in the case of unmannerly youths. Many lads who seem quite impervious to the infliction of cane or birch

CHILDREN'S AUTUMN DRESSES.

The Ladies' Treasury, 1859, III, 284.

11. Children's Autumn Dresses.

have yielded to the salutary restraint of the irksome stays. One great advantage such a system of discipline has, is in the fact that boys can be dealt with by the sex which thoroughly understands the mystery of busks and laces.

I am by no means a solitary specimen of a spell of tight lacing inflicted on me as a remedial discipline, and well I know its power for good. Up to the age of sixteen I was repeatedly flogged by my headmaster whose half-yearly reports of my bad conduct at last quite wore out the patience of my guardian. He then removed me from the school, and placed me at an establishment where great restraint was practised on the pupils. On my arrival I was immediately laced into an extremely tight, heavily-boned corset, fastened with a small padlock, and was securely locked in with a tiny key, which dangled among the jewelled charms fastened to the slender waist of the principal, a handsome widow, who was then about twenty-four. For nearly three years I was kept at this school, and I began to improve from the very first. The fair disciplinarian was very patient with us, but extremely strict. If she was displeased with us she would frequently tighten our corset with her own small, delicate white hands, and then, having made us prisoners with the dreaded key, would laughingly dismiss us, with a smart slap on our cheek, 'to play', as she mockingly suggested. Alas! we knew too well the extra tightening would condemn us to a day's almost sedentary occupation. I was soon a different lad under the dominion of my lovely mistress, who was ably assisted by her two pretty sisters, both of them younger than she was, but both admirable disciplinarians.

I went there a conceited, rough lad, and I left a perfectly obedient, polite youth, and I am quite certain I learned to respect authority as set forth in the form of a pretty woman much more than I used to do when mastered by the strong hand of my former master. Hoping you can find room for this.–Yours, etc. R.D.B.

The following 'Question', asked on 6 July 1889 (p. 297) seems a little far-fetched: 'Will any readers, ladies or gentlemen, who have been put through an involuntary course of strict figure training and been well disciplined by ladies, oblige by sending a full account of their training, with method and means used, to a lady who is going to start an educational home for youths and girls, where the strictest discipline and figure training will be enforced?–Mrs. Fischer, 25, Queen's-road, Bayswater.' In 1892, the occupier was Thomas Toschini, confectioner. In the 'Notes and Queries' section of 13 July (p. 314) 'R.M.' asked 'R.D.B.' to correspond with him on the subject of corset discipline. The next correspondent to enter the field was a woman, the first to advocate corset discipline for boys.

CORSET DISCIPLINE   31 August 1889, pp. 9-10.
I can quite endorse the opinion of several of your correspondents advocating corset discipline in the management of refractory children. A lady friend of mine has two daughters aged fifteen and sixteen with whom it has proved a complete success. They are both members of the tennis club to which I belong, and used to be much remarked by their rough behaviour, as they played more like schoolboys than young ladies. Their mother was advised to make them wear their stays while they played, instead of leaving them off, as they usually did; but she did more than this, by having them fitted with very long, heavily-boned stays, with stiff broad busks which, of course, quite prevented stooping, besides being very uncomfortable. They were laced very tightly when they next appeared, and I never saw girls so much improved, for they were now well-behaved young ladies. Their figures were slim-waisted and the lacing was so effective that, playing or sitting, they were obliged to keep erect. Their hands were encased in long, well-fitting kid gloves, which they were not allowed to remove. They now played a quiet, lady-like game, and looked very pretty and graceful, being laced so tightly that ungainly movements were impossible. Their mother says she finds this means of restraint is very beneficial, as it enforces patience and submission. When there is any

need for punishing either of them, it is easily done by tightening the culprit's lace so as to entail an extra degree of discomfort as discipline, as well as improving her figure and carriage. These girls never know now what it is to be without constant pressure and restraint, for at night their already slender waists on being released from their day corsets are immediately enclosed in others having flexible busks and laced in an inch smaller than before. Their hands are kept constantly gloved both day and night in very tight kid, and fastened by bracelets to prevent them being removed, and are becoming beautifully white in consequence.

I have carried out much the same system with my stepson, as he was very unruly, so at fourteen I subjected him to the regime of the stay-lace, and confined him in a long, stiff corset, which I tightened periodically, but, of course, never removed. He soon ceased to rebel, and has become a submissive subject to corset discipline, which renders impossible all unseemly indulgence of lolling about. As his stays are not allowed to be loosened, he has to exercise great self-control at meal times, being naturally rather greedy, and is consequently much improved in health. He is now nearly sixteen, and wears a beautifully moulded stiff corset 17 inches long, with a steel busk to prevent stooping. It clasps his figure tightly for its entire length, and only allows his waist to measure 18 inches. Of course this entails a certain degree of discomfort, especially during the night, but it is only what many girls have to submit to while they are at school, with the addition of backboards and stocks, which effectually sacrifices all ease and freedom. This discomfort is the important part of corset discipline, and must always be maintained, especially with boys, by tightening their stays periodically, for when he is under the regime of the staylace, and his figure enclosed in stiff unstretchable stays, he is easily made to submit to its being squeezed tighter and tighter, and by the irksome restraint which this entails he is constantly reminded that he is not his own master. In the case of a girl, her hands should always be tightly gloved in strong kid, and her shoulders firmly strapped back by braces in order to flatten the back. The compression of her waist should commence at fourteen, as if begun young no ill consequences will ensue from even the strictest figure training.

Can any reader tell me where the books on figure training, mentioned some time since by a correspondent, can be obtained, or any others on the same subject?–Yours, etc.   FINISHED FIGURE   Kensington, W., August 13.

The next letter in the same issue is dated somewhat earlier and was presumably held over until a suitable opportunity arose for inserting it. The writer criticises corset discipline, but recommends an even more bizarre procedure.

31 August 1889, p. 10.

I have read with interest, and some disgust, the numerous letters that have lately appeared in your columns anent corset discipline. Tight lacing to gratify personal vanity I can understand, though I deplore it, but tight lacing as a punishment seems to me to be senseless, barbarous, and injurious to health. A sentence in the letter of 'Experimentum Crucis' in your last [29 June 1889] suggests 'a more excellent way', both as a means of discipline and a promoter of good carriage. I refer to the old fashioned stocks and backboard used in the last generation to correct the bad habits (alas, still prevalent!) of turning in the toes and stooping. By the backboard, I do not mean the steel backboard and collar–that fearful instrument of our grandmother's days–but the more modern wooden instrument of that name. Perhaps some of your fair readers can give us their experience on this point, and tell us where these necessary articles can be procured, or mention any schools where they are still in use. Such information would be useful to many of us, who are, like myself,   OLD FASHIONED
July 1 1889.

The following week a similar letter appeared also condemning corset discipline, but recommending tight gloves.

7 September 1889, p. 25.

As a medical man I must utter my protest against the compulsory wearing of stays as a discipline for young people of either sex.

I am sure tight lacing must be bad for a growing boy's health. At the same time the theory is an admirable one, and with certain modifications, a most wholesome regime for a rough, conceited lad who should be made to feel that he cannot do as he likes.

Now I venture to affirm that what I may term glove-discipline provides a sufficiently irksome and restraining power for a disobedient lad, and for the time will prevent him running riot and using his boisterous powers in unmannerly ways.

Permit me to describe a part of my school routine which I went through some years ago at a very strict establishment.

The principal was assisted by his daughter, a young lady who, when I went, had not long left a finishing school in Paris. If we incurred her wrath she often ordered us to have a spell of discipline gloves. We then had to wear a tunic with the sleeves cut away at the elbows, giving room for a pair of twelve-buttoned tight pale kid gloves to be exposed to view. The gloves fitted us perfectly, and were carefully cleaned before we put them on.

We were obliged to keep them free from the least vestige of a stain, and this could only be done by sitting or standing quiet, or reading some book which was scrupulously clean.

The top buttons were tied with thin ribbon, and the knot sealed with a little wax, and stamped with the crest of our pretty tyrant. Woe betide the unhappy delinquent who did not keep the wax intact. If when we went to her boudoir for inspection she found we had soiled the kid, dire results overtook the culprit, for he had to hold out his palms to be slashed by a long birch rod consisting of three thin shoots bound together at the end with a piece of white kid to prevent her exquisitely soft white fingers suffering any inconvenience from the friction during the energetic exercise.

As a boy of eighteen I have begged my smiling executioner for mercy, as the pain was most severe. I can vouch for the success of the glove discipline, and I am confident it is far safer than the punishment of the corset.

We dreaded it, as it put a stop to our freedom for the time, and we were in fear of soiling the kid.

As a substitute and a useful one for the dangerous stays, I recommend for rude and rough lads the discipline of the gloves. I should be much obliged if you can insert this.–Yours, etc. P.V.S.

Even stronger criticism was printed in the next issue.

14 September 1889, p. 42.

I am not hopeful that the refined cruelty, so unseemly boasted of by 'Finished Figure' and her friends, will be stopped as a result of anything I or anyone else have to say, but will you allow me to protest as strongly as I can against its barbarity? Because, forsooth! a woman has lost control (if she ever had it) over her children, she must needs go and strap them in an instrument of torture! Was ever such a thing heard boasted of outside the walls of the Inquisition? Might I suggest as alternatives the thumb screw, the boot-jack, or even the body-rack as further aids to proper behaviour? Many of your readers know a little, at any rate, about physiology and anatomy. Listen, and imagine all that happens when 'F.F.' applies her treatment. Two young, healthy, jolly girls thoroughly enjoy a game of lawn tennis. Some wasps (i.e.

people with slim waists) suggest, and the mother at once agrees, to clap the girls in 'very long, heavily-boned stays, with stiff, broad busks, preventing stooping, besides being very uncomfortable'. This 'enforced patience and submission'. To punish them 'tighten the culprits' (a word quite in keeping with the savagery of the operation) lace so as to entail an extra degree of discomfort'. At night 'lace them in one inch smaller than before'. And what is one of the grand, chief results? No language can describe the horror with which I read it, knowing its meaning, 'they are becoming beautifully white'. The treatment of 'F.F.'s' stepson is brutal in the extreme. Does it not make one's blood boil to hear anyone talk so flippantly of brutalities worthy only of the thirteenth century? Talk about the open brutality that we hear so much about among the poor–for a specimen of the very essence of cruelty refer to the refined, modernised inhumanity of 'Finished Figure'.   W.A. DAVIDSON

Other readers did not share Davidson's disgust. In the 'Notes and Queries' section on the same page, 'Nursery Governess' has this Question:

Will 'Finished Figure' kindly give the readers of the FAMILY DOCTOR the benefit of her experience as to the best kind of gloves to be used in connection with the discipline corset, and the means employed to enable one to put them upon the hands of refractory young people. How are they secured against clandestine removal, and how often is it necessary to change them? As this kind of refined irksome restraint seems to be taking the place of the barbarous birch rods, any information as to its mode of application would, I feel sure, be most acceptable to the readers of the FAMILY DOCTOR.

In the 'Answers' of that date 'Finished Figure' received this reply from 'Well Laced'.

In answer to 'Finished Figure' she will find useful hints in a book called 'Corset and Crinoline,' published in 1865 [actually in 1868] from letters published in the *English Woman's Magazine* of about that date [i.e. *The Englishwoman's Domestic Magazine*]. There were some letters in *Modern Society* 17th August, one of which gave an account of some girls who enjoy perfect health and have beautiful figures although they bathe and do gymnastics in very tightly-laced stays [This information is correct].

Further evidence of the interest aroused by 'Finished Figure's' letter is provided by this item at the end of the 'Notes and Queries' section: 'NOTE.–Will "Finished Figure" forward her address, as a number of letters addressed to her are at the office.–ED. F.D.' 'Medicus Parens', this time giving the address of his club, then replied to the criticisms of 'P.V.S.' on 28 September 1889.

28 September 1889, p. 73.
I think your medical correspondent, 'P.V.S.' would somewhat modify the opinion he has expressed respecting the 'injurious' effects of corset wearing on growing boys, if he looks at the question from a different point of view. The class of persons dealt with are, *ex hypothesi* belonging to the upper ranks of society, and do not need to earn their bread by manual labour . The cultivation of athletics cannot, therefore, be put in comparison with moral benefits, such as a habit of obedience and the restraint of an intractable and, where it gets the opportunity, a tyrannical, frame of mind. The whole future of the boy is at stake, and it is not of the least importance whether he is or not one of the Oxford eight or the All-England eleven. That mischief can be done by tight lacing is, of course, possible; but it is wonderful how few genuine cases have yet been produced. Let it be recollected that there are at least five kinds of corset wearing–1. loose;

2. comfortably tight; 3. painfully tight; 4. injuriously tight; 5. dangerously tight. Of these the interval, from a physiological point of view, is considerable between each stage and the next. So that injury can only result from the deliberate ignoring of Nature's warnings unmistakably given.

I quite agree with the idea of the glove discipline; but 'six-button' gloves of any moderately light shade answer the purpose well; and it must be remembered that extreme particularity assumes a set of surroundings very difficult of attainment.

As for caning or birching the hands, there can be no doubt whatever of the injury thus liable to be done to a delicate and all important member of the body. But the same objection does not apply to the old fashioned method now being revived, which (unless the infliction is of a downright savage character, partaking more of passion than of discipline) has never within the memory of man done the smallest possible injury to either boy or girl.–I am, Sir, your obedient servant, MEDICUS P.
Imperial Club, 3, Cursitor street, W.C., Sept. 6, 1889.

There is now a short lull in the correspondence on corset discipline, although B.N. Serré of Queen Victoria-street did have this to say of it on 2 November 1889 (p. 154): 'As for the supposed cruelty of subjecting children to the discipline of the corset, in the hands of proper persons it is the mildest and most easily graduated means of reformation ever introduced, and may well replace the present hypocritical and ineffectual systems.' The subject is then reopened with this extraordinary letter from 'Trim Waist'.

14 December 1889, p. 250.
I have read with much interest the remarks of some of your correspondents on corset discipline. I agree with those who advocate a trim waist and neatly gloved hands. If to these adjuncts of dress dainty high-heeled boots are added, the effect of a pretty girl is simply charming. Now, sir, I am sure if you would see me you would endorse what I have said. I am a young lady who is called by her friends a very pretty one. My figure is extremely slender, my waist, under the power of the stay lace, measures seventeen inches. I wear delicate kid boots with heels four and a half inches. My heels [*sic*, but see her next letter] are exceptionally soft, and as white as snow, the size of my gloves five and a half. I wear the most perfect fitting thin French kids, and prefer the palest tints.

Six months ago I married a gentleman who was a widower. Soon after my marriage the thought struck me, why should not my stepson have some of the advantages which improved me? He was a most unwilling subject, but I forced him to wear high-heeled boots, and with my maid's help, laced him into a tight, heavily-steeled corset, drawing it tighter every day. I frequently order him to wear very tight kid gloves, and these I fasten on with leather straps, buckled as firmly as possible round his wrists. If he soils the kid I punish him by some tingling visitations of my gloved palms across his cheeks, or if the culprit deserves severer correction by some smart cuts on his hands with my riding whip. He is a youth of eighteen, and is rapidly being changed from a rough, unmannerly lout into a docile, obedient youth.

I make him attend on me, and am teaching him how to behave in a young lady's presence. At first he could hardly button my gloves without tearing them, and I had to make him practise on old soiled kids. Now he can fasten a new pair of tight gloves without injuring them.

I certainly am a strong advocate for corset discipline and its smart surroundings, not only in the case of girls, but for their brothers also. I hope this long letter can find a space in your nice paper.–Yours truly, TRIM WAIST

'Trim Waist' wrote immediately to correct the error in her first letter.

281—New Summer Costumes for Children

Egyptian girdles, Turkish jackets, Russian toquets. It becomes more difficult than ever to dress really well and in good taste, and to avoid those fashions which are too much exaggerated to be ladylike.

The materials most in vogue for dresses this season are mohair printed with coloured designs, chinel krep, toile de laine, with small coloured patterns, plain or striped; suitacin, a sort of very fine linen, with brocaded patterns. All these materials are, in general, light-coloured, grey, salmon-coloured, green, fawn, buff or lilac, with very small patterns or stripes, or merely chiné. These that are

12. New Summer Costumes for Children.
The Englishwoman's Domestic Magazine, May 1867, p. 257.

I daresay my own carelessness caused the amusing mistake in my letter of Dec. 14. Of course, I meant my hands, not my heels, were exceptionally soft and white. One reason why I wish to lay stress on the delicacy of my hands is because there is a mistaken idea with some opponents of the tight corset that it makes the hands red. My hands, in spite of my tight lace, are very lovely. The skin is as smooth as white satin, and I have soft dimples tinged with a tiny soupcon of delicate pink.

May I be allowed in your delightful paper to state that I am sure that nothing does a rough, unmannerly youth so much good as to be well corseted under the *régime* of a smart girl, who will not hesitate to bestow at times sharp discipline. My young gentleman improved in a marvellous manner since I took him in hand, and put him through figure training. He has always to be near to lace my boots, fasten my bracelets, and put on or take off my gloves, etc. As I wear them frequently indoors he has to glove and unglove my hands for meals, writing, music, etc. I am very particular as to the fit of my gloves, and he has to put them on my delicate taper fingers as though they were a second skin. If he leaves a wrinkle in the kid I make his face tingle for a long time. It is quite amusing to see how afraid he is when he has to manipulate a pair of my twelve button new white kids. Some people may think I am an exacting young lady, but I am certain my *régime* does the boy an immense amount of good. I take great interest in corset discipline, and though I do not wish to correspond privately, I hope some day to allude to the subject again.–Yours truly,   TRIM WAIST

As in the case of 'Finished Figure', the letter from 'Trim Waist' excited a lot of comment, most of it highly critical. 'Genteel', however, asked on 11 January 1890 (p. 314): 'Can your lady correspondent let me know what kind of high heel boots she put her stepson into? I can wear a 5 ladies' size.' And 'Juvenis' enquired on the same day: 'Can any of your readers inform me what make of corset is most suited for a boy of fifteen, and also the price of the same?' An unnamed correspondent advised these two on 1 February 1890 (p. 362) 'to go for gentlemen's and boys' stays, to Madame Norris, New Cross Road, S.E., and Cross Street, Woolwich. She has great experience in figure training, both boys and girls, combined with anatomical knowledge. I would also recommend "Genteel" to go to Mrs. O'Sang, 98 Wardour Street, who makes ladies' high-heeled boots for gentlemen.' The first to express disgust was 'J.J.M.'

Having been a great admirer of your very valuable paper for this past three years I am naturally very interested in every article, which you always deal with so splendidly; but being an ordinary man, and Englishman in every sense of the word, I cannot help but write to express my disgust at your correspondents, 'Trim Waist' and 'Modern' [the latter wrote about high heels, apparently for men, on 28 December 1889]. I cannot think that either of them are English, surely they must be some French or German embeciles [*sic*].

The idea of a man, such as 'Reformer' [21 December 1889, p. 267: see *Men in Petticoats* p. 15] speaks about, wearing petticoats, and also of a man wearing stays and high-heeled boots. Comment is unnecessary; such ideas are positively unnatural and disgusting, and do not speak much for the morals of the respective writers.

I should be pleased if you would insert this in your next issue.–I am, Sir, faithfully yours,   J.J.M.   Regent's Park.

'Genteel' received a direct reply from C.K. Bayly.

STAYS AND HIGH HEELS   25 January 1890, p. 345.
　　To 'Genteel'.

　　In answer to your letter published in the FAMILY DOCTOR of the 11th inst., if you forward me your name and address I can enlighten you on the subject, having worn both corsets and high-heeled boots myself for some years. I consider that I have greatly benefitted by wearing corsets. With regard to high-heeled boots, that is merely a matter of taste; but they are not hurtful if well and properly made. I shall be happy to give you any information on the subject upon communicating with me.– I am, Sir, yours truly, C.K. BAYLY　　28, Pembroke-square, Kensington, London, Jan. 12, 1890.

　　This is a genuine name and address, the occupier of number 28 in 1892 being Collins Kinnear Bayly. At the end of a long letter about spurs and dress for lady riders, 'Admirer of Pretty Feet' replied to both 'Trim Waist' and 'J.J.M.'

25 January 1890, p. 346.
　　You did me the honour some time ago of printing my views on the subject of corset discipline, and if 'Trim Waist', after turning back to the number containing my letter [8 June 1889], would like to ask for any further information I can afford, I shall be pleased to write again on the subject. Perhaps that young lady when she next writes will tell us whether she rides, and what are her views as to the spur question.

　　'J.J.M.' in his violent attack, confuses entirely what is a mere matter of discipline with effeminacy. If he would like to think a little he would see that there are no two things more utterly opposed. I would myself never think of wearing stays now or high-heeled boots, but as a matter of discipline as a youth I had to do both, and be in constant attendance upon a most exacting young lady, who never scrupled to inflict stinging punishment for trifling offences. So I approve of 'Trim Waist's' system, though I would agree with 'J.J.M.' if the lad laced for pleasure. An effeminate man I utterly loathe, but being disciplined by a smart girl is quite another thing.–Yours, etc.,
　　　　　　　　　　　　　　　　　　　ADMIRER OF PRETTY FEET

　　'Philip' also wrote a long letter about ladies' spurs (8 February 1890, pp. 378-9). At the beginning of his letter he has a word of praise for the paper and 'Trim Waist', in particular: 'Three months ago I bought by chance a copy of your paper, and ever since then I have been a delighted and instructed reader of it. Your correspondence columns I have read with great interest, especially the charming letters of the fair "Trim Waist", from whom I hope we shall soon hear again on the subject of figure training for youths.' 'Fanny', by this 'Question' of 8 March 1890 (p. 27) also appears to be sympathetic to 'Trim Waist': 'Having two unruly boys of thirteen and fifteen, will any reader kindly let me know where any of the following articles can be obtained: Long, stiff, well-boned corsets, backboards, stocks and collars?' 'Trim Waist' contributed a third and final letter in April.

12 April 1890, p. 105.
　　I should much like to add a few words to my former letter on figure training and corset discipline. My stepson has simply improved in a marvellous manner since I have exercised discipline over him, and, instead of stooping half double, holds himself straight as an arrow. I have on several occasions sent him to bed without unlacing his corset, which is fastened at the waist with a small padlock, of which I keep the key. I have reason to think this restraint at night is a real punishment, and one which he dreads.

　　My sister, who has lately left school, tells me that the majority of the young ladies at the fashionable establishment where she has been so perfectly trained sleep in their stays. Clara has always done so, and is the picture of health. She has a delicate complexion, a very slender waist, neat feet and ankles, and pretty, small, soft hands quite as white and lovely as mine. I never saw a more perfect beauty, she is simply bewitching. I am glad to say she is able to help me with my stepson's training, and gives him a daily dancing and drilling lesson.

Of course, the boy has to attend on her just the same as on me, and she is even more particular than I am as to the accuracy with which her gloves are fitted on her dimpled, snowy white hands. Clara is rather stronger in her dainty jewelled waist [*sic*, but obviously 'wrist' intended] than I am, and I often hand the culprit over to her for punishment. She does not hesitate to use her taper riding whip very freely on his gloved palms for the most trifling faults, and he is in very great dread of his lovely punisher.

I should like to add that Clara and I are very fond of riding, and never dream of going out without our pretty little spurs, which we use to make our horses give us plenty of invigorating exercise. It is a pretty sight to see my sister on her splendid horse, which she controls so easily by means of a sharp bit. Her exquisitely white kid gloved hand, though so small, easily restrains the strong animal and her little armed heel frequently stimulates his exertions.

Please try and find room for this, Yours truly, TRIM WAIST

It is curious that this letter contains the same sort of verbal error as her first letter. In that she put 'heels' instead of 'hands', in this, 'waist' instead of 'wrist'. This would suggest that the writer was at least someone outside the paper. The printing of the paper is of very good quality. There are very few printing errors. They also seem to print letters exactly in the form in which they were received, without changing words or paragraphing. What these little errors suggest to me is that the three letters from 'Trim Waist' did come from one individual who was not an employee of the paper. Whether or not the contents of the letters are true or the writer a woman is another matter. The next two letters are both concerned with corset wearing in Vienna and the third claims that no English boy would submit to the treatment of 'Trim Waist'.

19 April 1890, p. 124.
Here at Vienna, I see boys of ten and upwards well laced into tight fitting stays. From remarks I have overheard, it is evident they find them very comfortable. Certainly their figures and carriage are vastly improved. I should like to corset my own boys; can any of your readers who have actual experience in this matter give me some advice as to the best make, etc. Gentlemen's stays are becoming quite the fashion, they may be seen in shop windows and advertised in the papers.

Ladies like now to show the tiniest of waists. A friend of mine, who has excellent health, measures just 16 inches when laced, and finds it most pleasant.
MOTHER OF THREE BOYS

26 April 1890, p. 137.
I read in your journal 'Trim Waist's' letter on corset discipline, and as I have had some experience in these matters on the continent, I think it would be interesting to many of your readers.

Some little time ago I was living in Vienna and accepted a situation as governess in an Austrian officer's family. I had the charge of the two children–a girl of thirteen and her brother, aged eleven. The mother of them although rather short, had a very slim figure, and was a strong advocate of tight lacing. Her two children wore stays which I was expected to see were closely laced and fastened; besides this they always wore very nicely made boots and shoes with very high pointed heels. Once a week there came to the house a gentleman who taught them dancing and deportment, and it was part of my duty to see them dressed and got ready for their lessons. The young lady wore a short evening dress, and the young gentleman a black, tight-fitting velvet suit and knickerbockers. Both wore light kid

71

gloves and silk stockings, and high buttoned satin boots, made expressly for them with extra light French wood heels, very sloped under the foot, the base of the heel being very little larger than a sixpence. Their stays were laced in as tightly as they could bear them, and they had to keep in this same dress for the remainder of evening until ready for bed. Both wore corsets to sleep in.–Yours faithfully,   MARIE KRAUSE   Hanover Terrace, April 15, 1890

26 April 1890, p. 137.

I read with much interest and amusement the racy letter by 'Trim Waist' in your last issue but cannot help feeling that it was intended as a joke, unless, indeed, the stepson referred to is a mere baby; if not, I must (as one of the opposite sex) protest against his being taken as an example of English boyhood, for no English boy with manly feeling would submit to such effeminate treatment. For my own part, I am now only a young man, and can well remember my feelings as a boy. Then, as now, I had a great liking and admiration for the fair sex, and would not hurt them on any account; but it was, and is, the feeling of the stronger for the weaker, and in no possible circumstances would I use violence, but in many cases would use gentle force and determined resistance, and certainly would not have suffered the indignity of being laced in the effeminate article–a corset–not even if my stepmother had been assisted by three sisters, instead of by only one, as in the instance given.

Well can I remember an active cousin, assisted by three servants, attempting to bind me into a chair, but having to give in, notwithstanding I was only twelve years old, and my cousin a lady of spirit and strong will, who had determined she would do so. But this was a warning to her, and I hope, will be to others, not to determine too much in these matters; for it is in such that the determination of the tender sex fails, and their weakness becomes evident.

As to any benefit arising from corset wearing, I should think, as a general rule, it proves very beneficial to the sex, who, not having sufficient energy and staying power to hold themselves straight, need this discipline to keep their waists trim. Otherwise they would become flabby, and the curve, which in a good female figure is so decidedly the line of beauty, would no longer exist, but no man worthy of the name requires this artificial aid.–I am, Sir, yours faithfully,   NATURAL WAIST, April 16, 1890

There follow several more letters condemning 'Trim Waist', while 'Medicus Parens' argues for a more moderate application of corset discipline. Most contributors accept 'Trim Waist' at face value and do not question her veracity or sex. Two are puzzled by the verbal error, but are unable to think of the correct version.

3 May 1890, p. 154.

In reply to your correspondent 'Trim Waist', may I be permitted to express disapproval of her, to my mind, extraordinary conduct? Speaking of her stepson 'Trim Waist' writes, 'I have on several occasions sent him to bed without unlacing his corset, which is fastened at the waist with a small padlock, of which I keep the key.' This I would characterise as a refined species of unnecessary or senseless cruelty, and, if commonly indulged in, magisterial interference would soon be manifested. In this city, a little time ago, a father received 'six months' hard' for fastening his boy to an unused firegrate with a padlock.

'Trim Waist' goes on to say, 'I have reason to think this restraint at night is a real punishment and one which he dreads.' Well Mr. Editor, permit me to query the 'reason'. I have no doubt about the 'real punishment' neither had the delinquent to whom I have just referred, neither had the said delinquent any doubt about the efficacy of the restraint, although it was only practised by day. I consider 'Trim Waist' up to the present has been very fortunate in being able to pursue unchecked her unique kind of training for the young; perhaps, the privacy attending her conduct has been the means of shielding her from the consequences of her senseless conduct.

'My sister, who has lately left school, tells me that the majority of the young ladies at the fashionable establishment where she has been so perfectly trained sleep in their stays.'

Well, I, and I think ninety-nine out of every hundred young ladies, and I may say old ladies too, think it would be far more sensible and becoming if the young ladies at the fashionable establishment sleep in nightdresses, minus the stays.

'Clara has always done so, and is the picture of good health.' So was the young boy 'the picture of good health' whose father suffered six months' imprisonment; so are hundreds and thousands of the poor street Arabs, who are shoeless and stockingless the picture of health; but going without shoes or stockings in cold weather has no more to do with the picture of health than has sleeping in corsets or being padlocked to a grate.

'She has a delicate complexion, a very slender waist, neat feet and ankles, and pretty, small, soft hands, quite as white and lovely as mine.'

Surely to goodness, 'Trim Waist' does not think any young man would be so senseless as to marry such a one unless she had an ample fortune to compensate for all these drawbacks.

'Never saw a more perfect beauty, she is simply bewitching.' I respect the right of 'Trim Waist' to discriminate; but allow me to say, for Clara to be successful in the art of bewitching, she must do more than bewitch her sister; there must be taken into the reckoning the stern, commonsense judgement of the opposite sex.

'Dimpled, snowy-white hands.' Just imagine what kind of a helpmate such a one would make to millions of working men in this country.

'Clara is rather stronger in her dainty, jewelled waist than I am.' I have asked several of my lady friends, but none are able to tell me what that means. They have never before heard of a 'dainty, jewelled waist'. It is almost as great an abuse of language as to write abut a 'lovely punisher'.

In conclusion I feel constrained to say that, in my opinion, 'Trim Waist's' treatment towards young children and horses is not likely to remove the general unfavourable impression entertained towards stepmothers.–I am, Sir, yours etc.,

    ELIZABETH HENRIETTA HIGGINS   35, Ackers-street, Manchester.

This is a genuine address, although the street has since been demolished, off the Oxford Road in Chorlton-on-Medlock, Manchester 13. In *Slaters Directory of Lancashire and The Manufacturing Districts Round Manchester* of January 1890, Joseph Higgins is shown as occupier, but the Census Returns for 1891 give more information. They take us into the home of an actual reader of *The Family Doctor*. There were two households at number 35. The main one consisted of Mr and Mrs Higgins, two 'boarders' and a servant. Joseph Higgins had either died or was absent when the Census was taken on 5-6 April. Charles Higgins, aged 30, described himself as an 'author' and was born in Manchester. Elizabeth H. Higgins was aged 29 and came from Northamptonshire. The boarders were Lucy (?)Marshall, a widow of 47 from Glasgow, 'living on own means' and Frances Marshall, aged 23, apparently her daughter and not shown as having any occupation. The 'general domestic servant' was a girl of 16. The second household occupied two rooms and consisted of Gustav Hoffmann and his wife Jane, aged 29 and 25 respectively. Gustav was born in Saxony, Jane in Buxton. Both worked, he as a 'professor of music', she as a 'drapery traveller'. It is thus confirmed that Mrs Higgins was a young married woman as seems to be implied in her letter. As for Mr Higgins, there is one and only one entry for him in the Catalogue of the British Library: 'Higgins (Charles) Writer on the Irish Land Question. *The Irish land question: facts and arguments*. pp. 172. J. Heywood: Manchester, [1885].' Higgins would only have been 23 in 1885 when his single work of authorship was published. He must have had his 'own means'. All resident at number 35 must have enjoyed seeing Mrs Higgins' letter in print and reading the comments on it.

CORSETS AND SPURS 10 May 1890, p.169.

Allow an old-fashioned woman to ask. Do you approve of 'Trim Waist' and her supporters, who have been publishing their views in your paper more freely than what I call the 'common sense' party? I missed the first letter by her, but am shocked by the second; her poor stepson has not only to endure the indignity of corsets and punishment from the fair stepaunt's riding whip by day, but the corsets fastened with a padlock, of which 'Trim Waist' keeps the key, and sometimes it is her pleasure that he shall sleep so fastened up.

I have studied children's health, etc. for many years, reading any reliable book on the subject, such as Bull and Chavasse's. The latter gives an instance of a young woman who died, and her liver was found to be dented in, from the pressure of stiff stays! We read lately of a Miss Lacy, who swam a wonderful distance from the 'Quitta' wreck. I do not believe she could have done a fraction of that in tight corsets. All the most active girls I ever met have been those who wore sensible, easy clothing. Even easy stays hinder your breathing when exerting more than usual activity in climbing, running or riding. I swam once a short distance in all my walking dress, and was disappointed at my slow progress, even in stays comfortably easy. Just a belt affords support, and does not hinder the action of heart, lungs or liver. Modern readers would think too coarse the remark I have heard quoted as one made by Dr. Abernethy, so I will only say it applied to someone who felt ill after lacing herself into less than half the size Nature made her waist.

'Trim Waist' asserts that at the 'fashionable establishment' her sister has just left, 'many girls sleep in their stays'. I should like to know where that school is that I may avoid ever sending a girl there. A cynic might think Madam 'Trim Waist' wrote partly to advertise the charms of her sister, who, she says, is 'simply bewitching', etc. Is it possible that she is angling for a matrimonial prize for Clara? Furthermore, her style in riding seems to be of the kind called 'showing off'. A sharp bit, a pretty little spur, a splendid horse, and, again, the charms of her sister!

We used to ride without so much fuss about it, and though the girls now would despise our doings as 'hum-drum', we had plenty of fun and exercise, and we did not wear out valuable horses by keeping them always on the caper. It seems the fashion now to be cruel. Some of your correspondents write in praise of bearing reins and martingales as giving an 'extremely smart appearance'; in fact, that seems to be the only object in dressing themselves, their children, or relations, but such a system will certainly not improve the race of young England growing up around us.

Corsets and other kinds of discipline may make boys more like dolls–if that is desired–but we shall look in vain for the English boys who used to grow up to enter our Army and Navy, and cause the English name to be respected all over the world. Hoping I have not exhausted your forbearance, I remain, yours faithfully, PRIMROSE Gloucestershire

CORSET DISCIPLINE 17 May 1890, p. 186.

I regret to see the above expression (which I believe first appeared in your columns in a letter of my own) associated with questionable methods of procedure, and still more uncalled for criticism. Your correspondent 'Mrs. or Miss Higgins' is so wrath with the idea of obliging a lad to wear stays against his will, that she compares it to the padlocking of a child in an empty room without necessary exercise or care, and probably (if the case was investigated) with starvation and much other ill-usage. It is incredible that any magistrate should have regarded as criminal a parent who had only exercised his undoubted right of confining an unruly child. Corset discipline, properly so called, has nothing to do with cruelty, and simply replaces other more severe forms of restraint and punishment.

In the female sex vanity forms so powerful a motive that this means of control is seldom wanting in the case of girls who otherwise would be unmanageable. But in the case of boys custom forbids the best of all known means of inducing habits of obedience, order, patience, and gentleness. We are told *ad nauseam* that 'manliness' must be first cultivated, and should have the precedence over all other considerations. Abstractly, this sounds well, but in real life we are often obliged to sacrifice one advantage in order to obtain another. How often is a promising youth allowed to grow into an unrestrained ruffian, to break his parents' hearts, scandalise the neighbourhood in which he lives, and utterly ruin all his own prospects, in order that this fetish of 'manliness' may be duly propitiated. It is therefore a matter of common sense to set aside false sentiment, and give boys the advantage of corset restraint when their persistent intractability has defied ordinary measures.

Could not some of your correspondents who have seen schools of this kind in Paris or Vienna give us the benefit of their experience, especially as to moral results, and inform parents who have been exasperated by the canting inefficiency of so many domestic pedagogues, where they can obtain for their children a good carriage, good habits, and unwavering discipline? In other words, to give the address of schools where corset wearing is a fundamental rule which may never be disregarded.–I am, Sir, your obedient servant,   MEDICUS PARENS
London, May 1, 1890.

17 May 1890, p. 186.

Will you kindly allow me to express my entire approval of 'Elizabeth Henrietta Higgins's' condemnation of so nonsensical and ridiculous a letter as one signing herself 'Trim Waist' was foolish enough to write. It is about as silly an harangue as was ever committed to paper.

Does 'Trim Waist' consider it right and proper that members of the masculine gender should at certain periods of their lives be encased in corsets? For my own part, I should like to become acquainted with the boy who would submit to such idiotic treatment. As for Clara, she is more to be pitied than laughed at with her 'pretty, small, soft hands'. Truly a lovely specimen for a working man's wife. But perhaps she is intended for a prima donna? And 'Trim Waist's' hands are equally as ravishing as Clara is 'bewitching'. Truly a magnificent advertisement for 'Trim Waist' and Clara, and one which would figure splendidly in a *Marriage Herald* (on hand column). As for the poor boy who has been subjected to such barbarous treatment, he has my fullest sympathy.

As regards 'Trim Waist' and Clara (charming creatures), I leave them in the hands of someone with as much commonsense as displayed in the letter of 'E. H. Higgins' from whom, no doubt, they get as much sympathy as they deserve.–I am, Sir, yours etc.,   ONE OF THE STERN SEX

7 May 1890, p. 186.

I am an old subscriber to your paper, and often read with interest the correspondence, but up to the present have taken no part therein. I cannot refrain, however, from expressing the pleasure of seeing that at last one of her own sex has taken the trouble of replying to 'Trim Waist's' letters, which at first I considered a bit of sarcasm on the previous correspondence by some male creature, as I believed such senseless cruelty and unblushing egotism impossible on the part of a lady.

shaped in front; sleeves closed at wrists; double cuff. Casaque bodice of Algerian gauze, edged with marquise ruches.

1218.—Children's Costumes.

1. Toilet for a little girl from 10 to 12 years old. Muslin bodice or casaque, double-breasted, edged with a double ruche; the skirt of the bodice is open at the sides, with revers. Under-skirt of spotted muslin.

2. Costume for a little boy from 8 to 10 years old. Costume of white piqué; paletot in the English shape; collar, facings, and pockets edged with black braid, buttons and fastenings of passementerie. Hunting waistcoat without collar, fastened round the waist with a leather belt. Loose trousers, white gaiters.

3. Ball toilet for a little girl from 4 to 5 years old. Pleated muslin bodice, cut low and square; Valenciennes skirt looped up *à la* Pompadour by pinked-out satin ruches; satin rosettes and foulard under-skirt with a scalloped-out edge. Coiffure adorned with a puff of roses.

ALBERTA SEWING MACHINE.

OUR attention has been directed to the Alberta Sewing Machine of Messrs. Whight and Mann, 143, Holborn-bars. This machine, which is a lock-stitch on the Wheeler and Wilson principle, differs entirely in appearance from any others we have seen, and is fixed on a "tripod" table. The appearance is very elegant, and the machine can be placed in a corner of a room, and occupies far less space than ordinary machines. The Alberta is furnished with a convenient box for holding tools, cottons, &c., and when shut down looks like a handsome work-table. The legs, which can be had bronzed or gilded, protect the dress of the operator from oil, and stand more firmly

1217.—Little Girl's Ball Dress.

upon uneven floors than the four-legged machines can. The price is 6½ guineas on plain table, and 8½ guineas with handsome cover complete.

We are happy to announce to our readers that Messrs. Newton Wilson and Co., of 144, High Holborn, have brought out a button-hole machine at 15 guineas, the usual price of these machines being £34, and not £14, as printed by error in our August number. This 15 guinea button-hole machine is a boon to large families, and to dress and shirt makers. Another improvement we remark in this company's Queen Mab Machine. A new form of this pretty and useful little machine has been introduced, and while neater, prettier, faster, and more silent than the old Queen Mab, the new Queen is to be had at the old price, £3 3s.

"ADDITIONAL" HAIR.

A CURIOUS cargo has just arrived at Havre—a cargo of false hair, or rather real hair to be used falsely. The hair in question is almost all black, and consists in great part of scalps of Apanchos, Comanches, and other native Mexican tribes. When the French army was in Mexico many of the Indians fled in terror to get out of the way, but first hid in caves and woods the bones of their ancestors, and the trophies they had won in war. Among the latter none are more sacred than the scalps of enemies with the long hair attached. Some smart French speculators, by the aid of bribery, contrived to discover the sanctuaries where these scalps were concealed, and the result is a gain for France which will cause a fall in the price of false hair.

1218.—Children's Costumes.

I should like to add that the punishment referred to by your correspondent, 'E. H. Higgins' is richly deserved in this case, and an equal amount for the father if he is at home and cognisant of what is going on. I pity the hapless youth, who must have lost, if he ever possessed, a boy's natural spirit or courage.

Such so-called figure training may be very well for a few helpless, hopeless, useless creatures who loiter away their feeble existence dangling after and dancing attendance on 'dainty jewelled (?) waists', 'neat feet and ankles', 'dimpled, snowy white hands', and such like showy, but fleeting, attractions which 'Trim Waist' desires all should know she possesses in such profusion; but where are we to find our future statesmen, soldiers and sailors who have made the nation what it is, or our gigantic commerce be carried on, if such unmanly training for our youths be adopted and accepted as a model?–Yours truly, R. SEDGERWOOD
Central Club, Birmingham,
May 5, 1890.

CORPORAL PUNISHMENT 17 May 1890, p. 186.
About a year back there was a correspondence in your paper on the subject of corporal punishment. I have been away a long time, and was not able to read all that was said for and against it. Lately, however, I have heard that the use of the birch has largely increased in families and schools. Do any of your readers know if this is so? As I feel a deep interest in this matter I shall be glad if any who have experience in the subject will favour me with their address, as I am now engaged in collecting information.

I entirely concur with your correspondent, 'E. H. Higgins' in her remarks upon the barbarous 'corset discipline'. I was immensely pleased with her sensible protest against such horrible methods of discipline, if they can be called methods of discipline at all. I venture to think, that if 'Trim Waist' had tried the effect of the birch, granting that her stepson had offended, she would have done a more sensible, a more efficacious, and a less atrocious thing: and, moreover, 'Trim Waist' will do well to heed the by no means too severe sarcasm of 'E. H. Higgins' as to corsets generally.–I am, Sir, yours truly, J. ROSS London, May 3.

CORSET DISCIPLINE AND CORPORAL PUNISHMENT 31 May 1890, p. 217.
So J. Ross has revived the subject of corporal punishment in your excellent paper. He thinks that 'Trim Waist' should have 'birched' her stepson instead of punishing him by strapping his corset tighter. I ask what lad of any spirit would submit to the indignity of being whipped by a woman? I ask again how can anyone calling herself a lady punish a poor boy in such a cruel way as to lock him into tight unbending stays for hours at a time? In my school days we were drilled pretty severely, but were not tortured by the cruel corset. Whipping was administered when we misbehaved by the head governess, a dozen sound slaps being given in private on the usual part, or if the girl had been very naughty, perhaps eighteen or twenty. It would be interesting to read a letter written during the first few months of corset discipline by the victim on the subject.– Yours faithfully, ELIZA.

There was then another short gap followed by the most extreme of all the letters on corset discipline.

13 September 1890, p. 42.
I am a young lady who believes in having all things as smart as possible–a slim, well-corseted figure, well-gloved hands, and dainty, narrow-toed high-heeled boots, fitting with never a crease, and having a most acute dislike to being worried with the boisterous rudeness of rough, unmannerly boys. My step-mother, with whom I have

lived ever since I was quite a child (and I am now twenty-two) was most particular to have me cared for to the utmost at home first, then at school at Brighton, and lastly at a very strict fashionable school in Paris where figure training and elegant, refined manners were objects of the most constant solicitude. In Paris, too, I was taught to ride, not as I had been taught in England, but to show off my horse by means of curb and spur. A number of us went at a time to the riding school, where one of the most successful mistresses of the day instructed us. Sometimes we would simply ride out with her for practice, at others she would keep us in the school the whole time. We would be all mounted, and drawn up in line, and she would call one girl out into the centre and put her through a number of exercises. Then another girl would take a turn, and so on, and I think some of your readers who object to spurs would have been much perturbed had they been present, for certainly when once we were permitted to use them we never wore them for nothing. The most unpleasant part of our riding was when she made us sit well up, about which she was extremely particular. The mistress made us wear a backboard, which she strapped as tightly as if we were in the drilling room. To have to sit thus upon a plunging horse was most irksome , but no remonstrance was permitted, and we knew better than to get reported to our principal, so there was nothing for it but to submit, though our shoulders might ache all the rest of the day from the unyielding firmness of the straps. Still, unpleasant as this was to go through, it was well repaid by the gain in appearance, and I often think now, when I see girls in the Park riding all in a heap, how I would like to give them a little of the same improvement.

A little more than a year ago a nephew of my step-mother came to live with us–a rough, rude boy of fifteen, whose noisiness quite upset the comfort of the house. We were very glad, I can tell you, when his holidays were over, and when Christmas drew near we lamented that he would be back again. I was saying so to a young lady friend, when she laughingly suggested my trying 'corset discipline' and showed me the first letter of 'Trim Waist' in your number of December 14 last. I liked the idea, and that very evening read the letter to my dear step-mother, who approved of it highly. Next day my corset-maker arranged to assist, and our maid was taken into the plan. By the time he returned all was ready for him (including a new gut riding whip), and the very next day I took him out with me, and without a moment's warning walked him straight into the corset-maker's, and, before all the assistants and a lady customer and her two daughters, stated that I had brought him to be fitted with a corset. He blushed crimson, and, I think, would have been glad if he could have concealed himself under a chair from the smiles of the two young ladies just mentioned. We were taken to an inner room, and in a few minutes the principal herself came to attend to us. He was most loath to submit, but we did not heed his objections in the least, and before very long he was satisfactorily laced up in a very stiff corset which had been already prepared. The principal then took from a drawer a little steel belt, which she secured with a pretty little ornamental padlock, the little key of which she, with a smile, handed over to me, and I hung it upon my watchchain, where, I am afraid, it tantalised him more than if I had put it into my pocket. Then, after he had been carefully measured for more corsets, we sallied forth again. The next visit was to a fashionable bootmaker's, where he was fitted with one or two pairs of laced and buttoned boots and low-cut court shoes, all of tightest fit and highest heels. Then I made him, though much against his will, walk home in a pair with only slight heels, but which to him felt like mountains.

From that time I have kept him almost daily in his corset, which the maid laces, always bringing me the key herself, and in the house he has to always wear the high-heeled boots. For the sake of his hands I require him always to sleep in gloves, for which purpose he is furnished with six-buttoned kids, and also to wear them whenever he goes out of the house. A thing which he dislikes very much, but which I find is excellent for keeping him out of mischief if I am out for the whole day, is to make him wear a short-sleeved jacket and a pair of twelve-buttoned white kids, up the buttons of which a special coloured thread of silk is wound so as to tell at once if he has attempted to undo them. Then, when I return, I see if he has soiled the kid in the least, and if he has, then he regrets it.

The backboard and stocks I have also introduced, and at once make use of them if he slouches or is clumsy or careless with his feet. The fixed collar upon the backboard he finds (as I found it in my time) horribly uncomfortable, but I make him wear it for two or three hours. Some of his corsets I have had fitted with shoulder straps, and these I find very successful. By these means, and by giving him frequent dancing lessons and drilling, he has improved immensely. I have also adopted 'Trim Waist's' suggestion, and make him attend on me and fasten my gloves or boots, or do anything else I choose to tell him. I never hesitate to punish him if I think he deserves it. The backboard and stocks afford capital means of punishment, or I can set him something troublesome to do or a thousand things. But for a punishment sharp and quick and over in a minute I bring my palms to bear upon his cheeks, or for greater punishment I produce that gut riding whip, and slash him across his palms just as many times as I think proper. He sometimes has to attend my step-mother and me to the theatre, and always in his best corset with the shoulder straps drawn tight, and white kid gloves and high-heeled boots. More than once I have made him stand behind our chairs during the whole performance.

My friend who gave me the first suggestion has always taken great interest in the proceedings. Several times she has spent the whole of a wet afternoon in assisting me with a dancing lesson, she and I taking it in turns to be pianist, the other acting teacher, and at each change he has had to remove the gloves of the one going to the piano and fasten those of the one coming from it, himself remaining gloved the whole time.

I think now that I am entitled to speak from experience, and I can confidently say that I have found corset discipline a perfect success, as from a boisterous, clumsy, rude youth my pupil has, under my *régime*, become obedient, well-behaved, and graceful, and dances beautifully. I am sure any boy would improve if taken in hand intelligently by a girl who could control him, and force him to submit to her discipline.

I should just like to thank another correspondent for a hint about bearing reins, which I have adopted with great success for the pair of tall ponies that draw my phaeton–namely, to add a rein like circus horses have, going straight from the bit to the top of the saddle. This being added to the ordinary bearing rein, and drawn as tight as possible, looks awfully stylish. I always use it when I drive, but the combination must be uncommonly tiresome to the horses. I should like to see it to every carriage, as it looks so dressy.–Yours truly,   WHITE CAT

The letter from 'White Cat' excited a great deal of interest as well as much unfavourable comment. Meanwhile 'Notes and Queries' included this 'Question':

20 September 1890, p. 59.

I wish to place two boys (eleven and fourteen) in a school where they will be corseted, gloved, and put into high-heeled girls' boots. Some of your correspondents have described themselves as having been placed at such schools. May I ask them to give me, in confidence, the address of these establishments, so that I may write and gain particulars? Any information as to the best make of corsets, etc., or relating in any way to the subject of the corset-discipline as applied to boys, will be welcome. I shall be happy to correspond with anyone on this subject. Letters may be addressed to 'Mr. F.B. Carter, 39, Wiltshire-road, Brixton, London, S.W.'

A Miss Stubbs is shown as the occupier of 39, Wiltshire-road in *Kelly's London Suburban Directory* of 1892. Miss Stubbs is perhaps Carter's landlady. In the issue of the following week, 'E.H.B.', although he makes no reference to 'White Cat', describes treatment at the hands of his aunt in some ways even more extreme than that of 'White Cat'. He, alone of all the boys whose clothes are described in *The Family Doctor*, is actually made to wear a dress. He is dressed as a girl.

CORSET DISCIPLINE   27 September 1890, p. 73.
I have read with the greatest interest the letters which have appeared in your paper on this subject, and have been hoping to see one from some one who has been under the *régime*, but up to now none has appeared. It may therefore be of interest to your readers to hear from me a personal account of how I was treated by my aunt.

I was early left an orphan, and up to my fifteenth year lived with an uncle who then decided to go out to Australia, and consequently I was transferred to the care of my mother's youngest sister, a young lady of about twenty-five, living in the South of France. Although I was nearly fifteen when I went to live with her, I was small for my age and being fair and girlish-looking would more readily have passed for twelve or thirteen than my right age, and I was, I must admit, a rough, untidy boy.

The second day after my arrival, in the middle of the summer, my aunt called me into her room and said she had decided to alter the style of my dress (I wore a knicker-bocker suit), and handing me a blue serge sailor dress and a pair of richly-trimmed closed linen drawers, told me to go up to my room and put them on instead of my cloth jacket and knickerbockers. I was so astonished that I could only stammer out something about not wishing to be dressed like a girl, when my aunt took out of a drawer a very thin gutta-percha ladies' riding whip, and said she would be sorry to have to use it, but that she should if I did not obey her at once. Terrified at the sight of the whip, I went up to my room and made the required change, and I found that the skirt just hid the lace on the drawers, but that every movement displayed more or less of them. The same afternoon my aunt told me she was going to give me a lesson in deportment, and, ringing the bell, told her maid to fetch my corset. In a few minutes Mary brought in a stout corset, and into this I was tightly laced by the two after, I should think, at least a quarter of an hour's work. The feeling at first was dreadful, but I was made to walk up and down the room holding myself perfectly erect, and getting a smart cut across my calves with the whip every time I slouched in the least. After an hour's drilling I had to put on a pair of my aunt's white kid gloves, and was told if I soiled them I should have some cuts with the whip over my palms.

From that day I was a perfect slave to my aunt, who made me wait on her in every conceivable way, and for every fault did not hesitate to use her whip freely, sometimes on my hands, sometimes on my calves, and on particular occasions over my linen drawers, which of course, were little or no protection.

I do not wish to trespass any more on your valuable space, but if any of your numerous readers would like to write me privately on this subject I shall be very pleased to hear from them.–Yours truly,   E.H.B.
4, Ludgate-circus-buildings, E.C.

The occupiers of 1892 were Edward Walker, newsrooms; Bertram & Co., wine merchants; Wilson, Walker & Co., leather manufacturers. In the same issue incredulity was expressed about such treatment:

27 September 1890, p. 74.
I should like to address to you a few words respecting the letter of your fair correspondent, 'White Cat', whose ingenuity is interesting, spiced as it is with a dash of

cruelty. Is not the lady in question asking us to believe a little too much? The boy referred to by her is said to have been fifteen years old, rude and boisterous. The fighting
weight, if I may use the term, of such a lad, would, roughly speaking, nearly equal that
of the young lady herself. How, then, can we credit the account of the various
penances inflicted, to say nothing of this rude lad's being laced up by the maid. Is it
done by moral suasion or physical compulsion? Perhaps 'White Cat' will further
enlighten us. Her story: *Si non e vero; ben trovato.*–Yours obediently,   DUBITANS

The Italian quotation should read: *'Se non è vero, è ben trovato.'* It may not be true, but
it's a good story. 'White Cat' never did write again, in spite of further requests and letters
addressed to her. In the 'Answers' column of the same issue, the editor included this item:
'Letters are at this office addressed to 'White Cat' awaiting reply.–Editor (27 September 1890,
p. 74).' Three more letters critical of 'White Cat' followed.

4 October 1890, p. 90.
I have just been listening to a letter read by one of my sisters, and which appears
in your paper of the 13th inst. and is signed 'White Cat', the more appropriate signa-
ture to which would be 'Wild Cat'. If all she says is true, she is a subject fit to be dealt
with by the Society for the Prevention of Cruelty to Animals, her treatment of horses
being no less vile than her treatment of the unfortunate boy, who must be a poor creature to submit to it. Any boy of that age that I have ever known would have knocked
her down had she attempted to use such tyranny and violence. With regard to the tight
boots, they might lame him for life by causing corns, bunions, and other injuries to the
feet.
In conclusion, I may say that my sisters agree with me in thinking the two women
are brutes and the boy an ass for putting up with such treatment.–Yours,
A READER OF THE FAMILY DOCTOR
Sept. 20, 1890

18 October 1890, p. 122.
I always take in your most valuable paper, and I have read with great interest the
numerous letters appearing weekly in your paper under the heading of 'Corset Discipline'. On the 13th of September a letter appeared signed 'White Cat'. I just wish to
express my opinion as to what I think about that poor unfortunate boy who, she states,
obeys her in everything, even in wearing corsets. I am a boy of fifteen, and would very
much like to see 'White Cat' putting me in corsets. I think it would be rather a hard job.
I do not think 'White Cat' would try it on again. If all she says is true, the boy must be
mad to put up with such treatment from someone only seven years his senior, if she is
only twenty-two as she says. But you know, even 'White Cats' would be likely to take
off seven years or so. I strongly agree with your correspondent who signs himself 'A
Reader of the Family Doctor'.
Hoping I am not too late for this letter to appear, as I should like 'White Cat' to
read what I think of her and her doings.–I remain, Sir, yours truly,
A BOY OF FIFTEEN
Twickenham

18 October 1890, p. 122.
After perusing the letter in your admirable paper from the correspondent who
signs herself 'White Cat', it struck me that her main object was to show what a large
amount of sense and ingenuity she possesses. It seems a pity that, if what is contained

14. Costumes for Children from Three to Twelve Years.
La Mode Illustrée, 18 August 1872, p. 258.

in her letter is true, she cannot put her inventive genius to some better use. It is difficult to believe that a lady of twenty-two years should write such a letter, abounding, as it is, in whims and ideas of the most ridiculous sort.–I am, Sir, yours,

COMMON SENSE
Windsor, October 5, 1890.

ANSWERS: 18 October 1890, p. 123.
    Letters at the office for 'E.G.N.' and 'White Cat'.

Several of the male critics of 'White Cat' and 'Trim Waist' thought a boy of fifteen should have been able to resist the imposition of the corset. Two previous correspondents imply that this would be impossible. At the end of a letter about 'Tight Boots', 'Eperon' says this:

13 December 1890, p. 250.
    I would here like to add something upon the subject which you now usually head 'Corset Discipline', but my letter is too long for much. I will only say here that although the impossibility of retaliation renders it wrong to place a lad under the power of a governess of cruel disposition, who will use her power badly, it is no reason why a proper custodienne should not exact that obedience to her decree which she is entitled to demand, and which it is most improving to a lad to have to yield.

'Curb' put this point even more clearly at the end of a long letter on gloves:

18 April 1891, p. 107.
    By the way, one of your correspondents lately suggested that a young gentleman page might not stand the 'joke' of punishment at a young lady's hands. Does he suppose that the lad is to punch a young lady's head as he might that of some turbulent schoolfellow? Surely the privilege of her sex is to be considered, and, then, how can violence on the boy's part be justified? I would not have a boy effeminate by any means, or apt to be bullied by his companions, but in attendance on a lady his submission should be absolute, even though she may exercise a little pretty tyranny, as from my own experience in that position, I know may be the case.   CURB.

The next two contributors to comment on 'White Cat' suggest that boys in that situation get to like their corsets. In the middle of a long letter on 'High Heels and Tight Lacing', printed immediately after the letter from 'Curb' just quoted, 'N.D.' inserted this paragraph: 'Readers would like to hear further of "White Cat's" boy in the knickerbockers, corset and high heeled boots. Some correspondents doubt her word, and, indeed, there seems to be only two explanations. Either "White Cat" is a veritable virago, or, what is more likely, the boy by habit got to like high heels and corsets.' 'E.G.', writing generally about 'Advances in Tight Lacing', made this reference to 'White Cat'.

4 July 1891, p. 283.
    I should like to ask some of the pretty stepmothers or 'White Cats' who so cleverly entrap rough and unruly boys into stays, and thence without resistance into collars and backboards, tight boots and gloves, and make them obey all their orders, how they educate them intellectually after they are too old for a ladies' school. A gentleman of experience tells me that we need not pity them, for they probably soon get to like it, as he did, and was a voluntary, though not constant, tight lacer at a large school, and at college, and afterwards, though he was strong and active and a 'reading man' besides. After giving it up for some time, he resumed it to cure indigestion with complete success, and after a few months found his waist several inches smaller than it had

been before he wore such long stays, and wooden busks as long and wide as possible, every morning, instead of only casually as he did when young.

Many persons think that the visible decline in the general size and health of boys and young men, while girls seem to improve, is due to early over-eating, aggravated afterwards by smoking. If so, it is clearly an additional reason for making them wear tight and stiff stays and busks, which soon makes over-eating impossible, or so unpleasant in its results that they cease to have any inclination for it. They may well relax altogether in the afternoon for athletic games, though not for ordinary walking. It seems that in Austria they are corseted from ten years old, boys no less than girls, and enjoy it, and young men in Prussia.   E.G.

The next correspondent was not put into corsets until he was seventeen, but he was brought into subjection by his stepmother and whipped by her. His letter therefore contains features which we have seen before. He also takes up the theme of over-eating.

TIGHT LACING   18 July 1891, p. 315.
The interesting correspondence on the subject of tight lacing will, I am sure, do good by the publication of the experiences of some of your readers. Of course, the lacing has in some cases been abused and much harm done by those who are ready to sacrifice health to appearance. At the same time I can bear testimony, as one of the male sex, to the excellent results of using the corset in a proper and legitimate manner.

As a youth I was very awkward and stooped in a way which vexed my guardian, who could not make me hold myself as I should. At the same time I was extremely greedy, and was always getting rich cakes and pastry when I went near a confectioner's. This state of things went on till I was seventeen. At that time my guardian married a young lady who had just left a very fashionable finishing school. Her waist was a marvel–only fifteen inches–and yet she had a splendid figure, and was rather over the average height. Certainly the tightness of her corset did not injure her health.

Mrs C. had a lovely complexion, and was fond of all sorts of out-door exercise. She was a magnificent rider, and her slender waist looked very trim and neat in her dainty habit. She liked the vigorous exercise caused by her powerful horse bounding and capering under the persuasion of her armed heel. I often wondered how (even with the help of a severe bit) her pretty, soft little hands could manage to keep him in such perfect control.

The young lady was also a great hand at tennis, and was most successful, though playing in a corset which made her figure perfect.

Soon after the young beauty came on the scene a change began to be effected in my appearance. I am now able to express my great gratitude for the common sense and firmness with which the lady treated me. There was no unnecessary severity, but I had to submit to a series of excellent regulations which soon improved my figure, and put an end to my greediness. Every morning a maid drew my corset as tight as possible. The first week it was drawn an inch tighter every other day. Of course I did not like it, but I dared not resist as Mrs C., though very patient, was a firm disciplinarian. I remember the second week trying to bribe the maid not to lace me as tight as she was ordered to do. Well do I remember the punishment I got from a certain little stinging riding whip. It did me good, and though I several times afterwards had a similar treatment for other faults, yet I was wise enough to submit to the lacing without any more open resentment.

The firm corset soon began to put a limit to the excess of my appetite, which was compelled to be moderate, and therefore a more healthy one. I was forced by the long, strong corset to hold myself upright, and, in fact, I became more inclined for exercise than in my slouching period of freedom.

I am now twenty-two, and look back with gratitude on the two years of an admirable system which, in my case, set me up and restored me to vigour and smartness. I think facts are worth so much more than theory, and hope you will find room for my practical experience.–Yours etc.,   D.M.

P.S. I should like to add that the lady is now a mother of two extremely fine children, and her waist still takes a fifteen-inch corset. She is the picture of health, and anyone would take her for a girl of nineteen instead of a matron of twenty-three.

Although the next letter is really outside our main theme, it does give some interesting information about a definite period forty-five years before. The youth concerned is made to wear stays by a woman–for his health, not as a punishment.

MALES WEARING CORSETS   29 August 1891, pp. 411-2.

I have long been a reader of the FAMILY DOCTOR, and take an interest in the corset question. Some time ago, a correspondent, signing himself 'Weak Lungs', wrote asking the experience of any male who had taken to wearing stays for that complaint. I may say that fifty years ago it was not considered effeminate for men to wear stays–it was quite common. Stay-making was mostly in the hands of men and John Smith, French stay-maker, was as common as John Smith, tailor. In the country these two trades were often combined.

I was brought up in a small town by the sea [presumably St. Andrews]. It was the seat of a university, and had a large boarding establishment for young gentlemen. When they went to bathe in the sea they took turns in lacing each other's stays when they came out of the water, and many a time I have had a stray sixpence for doing that service. At the parish school the boys whose parents were in a better position and able to afford it wore stays as a part of their ordinary clothing. They had to stand a good deal of chaff from us who belonged to the poorer class who could not afford to wear them, but it was mostly from envy. A present of a cast-off pair was much thought of. Young men, when they got to earning money, lost no time in getting a pair of stays. I had no stays myself until I was about the age of seventeen. About two years previous I had caught a cold, and was under medical treatment. I had grown very rapidly after getting my teens, and did not carry strength with it. I had a stoop in the shoulders, a narrow, contracted chest, a bad cough, and being an only son I was causing great anxiety to my mother. The winter was coming on, and my condition was by no means happy.

While I was dressing one day a lady come [sic] in about some sewing my mother was doing for her, and seeing I had not stays on, she asked my mother why she allowed me to go without them being so tall and delicate. Mother said I would not have them. 'Nonsense,' said the lady, 'he must wear them; why, he is getting all crooked for the want of them. I have a pair at home that were got for my son when we were in Paris some years since; they will fit him, and I will bring them over tomorrow.' She did so, and I had to put them on, for she would take no denial. The shape was what is called the long V, very deep in the front and back, but scolloped at the sides where they came over the hip bones; they were quilted with whalebone and steel till they were as stiff as a board. She did not lace me quite close at first, but I must say that I felt an amount of comfort I had not the least conception of. I persevered, and at the end of a week I could wear them laced quite close from top to bottom, and then I felt a feeling of perfect comfort and pleasure known only to the stay-wearer when laced into a pair of stiff, well-fitting stays.

I recovered my health rapidly, and grew broad-shouldered and straight. I have worn stays ever since, now forty-five years, and no man could have better health than I have. I still prefer the old-fashioned lacing stay, with strong busk and well boned.–Yours, etc.,   JOHN SULLIVAN   Portobello, Aug. 15, 1891.

I have already quoted a passage from a letter from 'E.G.' (4 July 1891). He wrote frequently to the paper on stays generally. This is the beginning of a letter under the heading: 'A Bearing Rein for Stooping Boys'.

16 January 1892, p. 313.

Ladies like the 'White Cat' [13 September 1890] and the stepmothers who educate rough and clumsy boys into smart and well-behaved young men by corset discipline may like to hear of a simpler and easier method of holding their heads up than the collars and backboards which many of them use now, or the still severer old ones such as the celebrated Mrs. Somerville suffered in at school [Mrs. Mary Somerville (1780-1872), a reference corrected and amplified in a letter of 6 February 1892 from 'J.W.B.' See also her autobiography (1873)].

Make a leather band about two inches wide large enough to fit close round the head like the lower part of a cap, nearly down to the ears. For wearing out of doors it may be completed into a covered cap. Fix a thin strap to it behind and fasten that down to the top of the stays as tight as will hold the head well up, and the business is done. Heads of some shapes may require a chin-strap from the front part of the cap to prevent it from being slipped off.

If the boy will not keep his hands off it they may be put into thick gloves holding the thumb and fingers together, or if that is not sufficient, button him up in a jacket with sleeves stiffened with a few laths or steel wire, which make it impossible to bend the elbows.

The same may be done for girls by weaving some silk strings into their back hair and tying them down to the stays. When the boys' stays are worn within the shirt it is better to cut a hole therein a little below the neck for the strap to go through than to put it inside the collar, which it will drag unpleasantly out of place.   E.G.

On 28 September 1889 'Carl' of Camden-square, N.W. had written describing how he had trained his daughters' figures with backboards and stocks. He now writes again in response to requests from other readers to give a progress report. Two of the daughters are married and have subjected their husbands to the staylace: 'He has submitted willingly to her imperious control'; 'she too induced her husband to become an ardent votary to the silken lace somewhat early during her engagement'. His last paragraph is as follows:

9 April 1892, p. 90.

I am happy to inform 'X.Y.' and also 'J.W.B.' that I know of several families in which the backboard and its accessories have been revived, and for girls (and young boys up to thirteen or fourteen years of age if unruly) I cannot conceive any less painful or more judicious method of imparting a graceful and refined carriage or demeanour, and a sense of submission to those in authority in the home.   CARL
Camden-square, N.W. March 26, 1892.

I have already quoted part of a letter from 'Curb' (18 April 1891). A year later the paper printed a long letter from him and he became the last major contributor on this subject.

THE CORSET AS A TRAINER   7 May 1892, pp. 154-5.

Whilst so many gentlemen are giving their experience of the benefits derived from the use of the corset voluntarily, I trust that one who has derived at least equal advantage from its use, at first under compulsion, may also be allowed to address you.

Up to the age of fourteen I had never worn stays or anything of the kind, nor, unless I had been forced to do so, should I have taken to them at all. Although I was a small, slim, fair boy, I was by no means mild of mood, but, on the contrary, was a perfect torment of mischief. My parents moved me from one school to another in the vain hope of finding one where I should be broken in, and were quite in despair what to do, when they were at length advised to try the effect of placing me with a lady who made an especial study of such cases, and had under her care about a dozen young gentlemen, whom she kept in the very strictest control. After anxious consideration, it was determined to try the experiment, and the lady who had given the advice was allowed to carry me off and deliver me over to her friend, I supposing that I was only going down to the country for a few days of holiday visit. The hostess, whom alone I saw on the evening of my arrival, was a pleasant-looking lady of about forty, or a little more, though her slim *bien corseté* figure made her appear younger, and she particularly delighted me by the agreeable interest she took in learning all about my school tricks and mischiefs, which I am afraid I rather magnified, little suspecting how nicely I was letting myself in.

The next morning on rising I found to my surprise that all my clothing except a few under articles had disappeared. After I had waited some time in these wondering, I was all at once surprised to see walk in an elegant young lady whose ankle skirts displayed the most charming pair of kid and patent leather *bottines* pointed to a degree, and who was followed by a maid bearing what I foresaw was to be the rest of my attire, and the young lady proceeded to give me her orders in an imperious manner that almost took my breath away, and almost before I could realise the situation I found myself being laced up in a corset of the most extreme stiffness, the discomfort of which was by no means lessened by the tight fastenings of a pair of shoulder straps. I begged to have these loosened, but the only reply was that if I were not quiet they would be tightened still more. A bright metal belt was then secured over the waist of a white flannel blouse, which was put over my corset, and the key handed to the young lady, who added it to several similar keys which I now saw depending from a bracelet upon one of her pretty wrists. A pair of white kid gloves were then put on my hands, and a thread placed so as to show if I attempted to remove them. Finally, the maid produced from a box a beautiful pair of high-heeled boots, the exact counterpart of those of the young lady. I had somehow been secretly nourishing a vain idea that I could hide from observation that I had on stays, and the gloves also I imagined I could conceal, but the boots there could be no concealing, and the sight of them aroused me to refusal. Upon this the young lady produced from a fold in her skirt a light-looking whip of gut, but which was so constructed as to be far more severe than might be expected. A few repetitions of her command, each enforced with a stinging cut that almost brought tears to my eyes, secured the required obedience, and I found myself as high-heeled and pointed-toed as my pretty commander, though the boots seemed to my unaccustomed feet by no means so easy for graceful movement as she evidently found them. I was then marched down to the hostess for her inspection, and she expressed her approval of my appearance, but on hearing of my refusal to put on the boots when first told to do so, she drew from a drawer a much heavier whip than that I had tried upstairs, and told me that a dose of that would be the consequence to me of getting reported by the young lady for disobedience. I was then dismissed to the playground with the information that the others had all breakfasted, and that I did not require any.

In the playground I found my future school-fellows–a number of lads mostly about my own age, but none younger. They were all in grey knickerbocker suits, with brown stockings and plain Oxford shoes. From them I learned that I was in what was called best drill costume which all wore once a week, and newcomers continuously until somewhat broken in. I also learned that I should in time come to feel no dislike to it, and I was warned that the most implicit obedience was exacted, and that all rudeness or noisy or rough behaviour was entirely prohibited. The young lady who had taken me in hand that morning, I was told, was madame's eldest daughter, who about

285.— Children's Costumes.
(Paper Patterns of Madame Goubaud, 30, *Henrietta-street, Covent Garden.)*

15.   Children's Costumes.   *The Englishwoman's Domestic Magazine*, July 1875, p. 32.

a year ago had taken the chief assistantship in succession to a considerably older lady, who had not been allowed nearly so much power as her young successor. Those who remembered the change said that the discipline was much more strict now than formerly. There was a second mistress, who, though several years older than the young chief, was not permitted to use a whip, but had to complain of our disobedience to get us punished. It was expected that before very long she would be dismissed in favour of madame's second daughter, who, having recently completed her education, now frequently assisted in the pupils' lessons, especially drilling and dancing. She was fully as stylish as her elder sister, and being at only seventeen permitted absolute authority over a number of boys all as tall as herself, several as old, and some even older, it is not surprising that she made a rather severe task mistress.

The very first morning when the school was called in I was left alone in the playground to receive from this young lady a drilling lesson all to myself. It was simply a marvel to myself how, in marching up and down that piece of asphalt, I learned as fast as I did to walk in the manner required of me, and I must confess that the result never would have been so rapidly attained but for the persuasive arguments now and then addressed to my calves. At the end of an hour she left me, having first summoned a maid to bring a backboard, which was strapped on me, and then the collar raised so that I could not look down at my feet when she was not there to look after me.

Tremendously strict as was the *régime* at this establishment, we were on the whole very happy, and I can certainly affirm for one that immense benefit was derived from it. In spite of the tyrannical exactness of our imperious young rulers, against whom there was no appealing, we had the greatest affection for them, and even if, knowing that their sex and personal advantages secured them from retaliation, they sometimes, when we were left in their sole charge for a day, permitted a pretty girl's natural love of power to somewhat stretch their consideration for us beyond what we thought quite kind, it was impossible for us to bear them any ill-will.–Yours obediently,   CURB

This letter from 'Curb' initiated a final phase in the correspondence. As a victim he was not criticised himself. Some correspondents asked for further information, others contributed narratives of their own experiences, previous correspondents and 'Curb' himself wrote again.

21 May 1892, p. 186.

As a parent, I owe a debt of gratitude to 'Curb' for his valuable information in reference to the breaking-in of unruly boys by the use of wholesome restraint exercised in a judicious manner.

I have two sons aged sixteen and fourteen who are being educated by my daughter's young governess, who is rapidly improving their recent rough and unmannerly behaviour. Mademoiselle is a strong believer in the power for good which the restraint of the corset can effect in the training of boys, and her charges are already–after only a few months of her treatment–wonderfully smartened up.

We have both read 'Curb's' letter with interest, and the pretty martinet has already acted on some of the hints gathered from that gentleman's past experience.

'Curb' would confer a great obligation on some of your subscribers if he would supplement his letter by some additional information concerning the discipline he went through. As I am anxious that the boys should receive the best correction from the young lady, I should like to ask 'Curb' to tell us something more as to the use of the whip at his school. Also whether his young rulers used their palms on his face, and, if so, with what success. As in the case of Mademoiselle, I am doubtful whether a girl with pretty, small, soft hands can hurt a big boy without the aid of a whip. Perhaps 'Curb' will enlighten us on these matters.–Yours faithfully,   D.S.

Will 'S.H.' give advice to the unfortunate guardian of two nieces, fourteen and seventeen years of age, who are absolutely beyond the control of their governess. Their brother, aged twelve, causes nearly as much trouble. The governess is altogether unable to cope with them. The girls are rebellious and defiant, and do pretty much what they please. They take all sorts of liberties with their brother and each other impossible to describe.

Glove and corset discipline have been attempted with the boy, but it has not been found practicable to carry it out. Directions or advice as to administering the birch or cane would be thankfully received. 'S.H.' may rely on the strictest confidence.–Yours etc.,   J. DERING   2, Hanway-street, Oxford-street, W.

As we have seen the latter is an accommodation address. Both these last two writers are probably just trying to elicit intimate details of punishment from 'Curb' and other readers. This 'Question' of 30 July 1892 (p. 348) was probably also just invented to invite a letter: 'Would any lady reader undertake the figure training of a young gentleman who belongs to a male dramatic club, and being of slight build, has promised to take a lady's part? Reply to "P.H.A."' 'X.Y.Z.' provided new information.

Noting in a recent issue an inquiry for information about the 'sliding neck collar' and other aids to the development of female beauty, I would beg to be allowed space for reply, having had much past experience of such instruments of discipline.

The collar and backboard I consider by far the most powerful and beneficial aids that can be fitted to any young person, whether male or female, presupposing that a corset is already fitted, of course. The backboard is much less dreadful to wear than its looks would suggest; in fact, after the first shock of its extreme rigidity has been overcome, it is much more comfortable than the elastic chest-expanding braces of the present day, which cut one so fearfully under the arm-pits.

The backboard, which is really the foundation of the apparatus, may be made of either wood or metal, a thin, stiff plate of steel being the neater for constant wear. It should be made the width of the shoulders at the upper part, and should taper downwards to less than the width of the waist, afterwards widening out again, and it should in every part be closely moulded to the figure in such shape that the chest is thrust forward and the body held erect. At the waist and at each shoulder a broad padded strap is inserted by which it is secured to the wearer. When strapped to it, there should be, if properly fitted, a feeling of absolute impossibility to bend anywhere except at the hips. The backboard should be covered with leather, and at each side of the centre outside, and close to the bottom, should be added a small flat staple for the insertion of a strap, which may often be useful to secure behind him (or her) the wrists of an unruly wearer who refuses to undergo the full course of discipline. My own little wrists, I may add, spent many weary hours in this position when I wore my first backboard.

Now for the collar, the most useful part of the appliance. This is a ring of steel which encircles the throat, and opens with a hinge at the rear. In front it has a lock and a padded chin rest. At the rear, just by the hinge, it is fixed to a vertical steel rod, which slides up or down as required in a locking apparatus fixed upon the backboard about the shoulder line. An apparatus exactly like this I wore constantly for over three years, and was often punished by confinement in others much more severe. As a boy I was most unruly, and even dirty, and a source of great trouble to all my family. After every means of domestic correction had been ineffectually exhausted, I was sent, at the age of eleven, to a ladies' school in the east of Scotland, the principal of which was known by certain friends of ours to be most severe in her treatment. She received only girls, but undertook my cure, I believe, at special solicitation and in return for offers of very handsome payment. However, here I was taken, and it was just such a backboard as the one above described to which I was secured, even to the wrists, in the presence of my own dear mother, whom, I can even now remember, laughed most heartily when she saw my violent struggles calmly overcome, and myself placed in the stocks with my face to the wall. I remember, too, that I was considerably astonished when I comprehended that instead of taking the house by storm, as at home, I had to endure my penance until completely tired of the position.

The 'stocks' in which I was placed were simply a wooden gutter which admitted the feet–placed heel to heel and held in a straight line–and secured them by means of a lid which shut down and had apertures for the ankles. The patient has to stand in them, and the toes are, of course, forcibly turned outwards. This course of treatment was continued for about a month with very, very short intervals.–I remain, yours etc.,

X.Y.Z.

In the final paragraph of a further letter, 'Experimentum Crucis', who says he is thirty-eight, gives more details of his early life:

8 October 1892, p. 91.

As a youth, with a weak back, I well remember the great benefit I derived by being trained under the care of an experienced lady with the corsets, backboard, collar, stocks and various other appliances. The discipline was hard to boys at first as it prevented much ease, and our diet was naturally restricted; but it did us much good, as we had to render absolute obedience to the ladies of the establishment where we were placed. The appliances which we almost constantly wore could be tightened or raised to a very uncomfortable height and securely locked upon any slight breach of the rules, which were most strict.   EXPERIMENTUM CRUCIS

The experiences of the following new correspondent at an Austrian school echo those of 'Walter' (*E.D.M.* Nov. 1867).

TIGHT-LACING   7 January 1893, p. 300.

I hope you will permit me to join in the very interesting subject which from time to time has been going on in your paper in reference to tight-lacing.

Some of your correspondents in this controversy pit Nature against Fashion, as though Nature must not be added to for the sake of improving the figure. I do not suppose, however, that these opponents of the corset object to the fair sex arranging their hair in a way which Nature has not done for them, or piercing the ears for the sake of adornment. Sentiment does not come into the discussion. What we want is practical experience for or against the use of the lace. I have worn corsets since I went to school in Austria. There the corset is drawn much tighter than it usually is with us, and the result is most pleasing. Both sexes lace up tight, and nearly all the Austrian officers and the majority of civilians lace up by no means loosely, and have smarter figures than Englishmen. At the age of sixteen I was sent to a school in Vienna kept by a retired officer. All his pupils were required to wear stays, and though, as an English lad, I did not like the idea at first, I never suffered any harm, and soon learnt to hold myself as upright as the other pupils. A smarter set of youths could not have been found than my school-fellows, and during my three years stay at the school I improved not only in appearance but also in health.

My appetite soon became more moderate, and, though I enjoyed the plain and excellent food, I rapidly lost my taste for sweets and rich things. I shall never forget the exquisite figures of the principal's two pretty daughters, who used to vie with each other as to who could have the slenderest waists and the most perfectly-gloved hands.

Some opponents of tight-lacing make the objection that a narrow corset results in pale complexions and red hands. I only wish such objectors could have seen those two Austrian beauties.

When I first went, the youngest was nearly seventeen, and, though she boasted that her waist only measured fourteen inches, her complexion was lovely, and her small, soft, white hands were like white satin.

Her sister, three years older, had a fifteen-inch corset and exquisitely-pretty fair hand, and a brilliant complexion. Their gloves were of the thinnest pale kid, fitting without a wrinkle.

Since I left school I have never ceased to wear firm, strongly-boned stays, which do not prevent my joining in energetic exercise. The rest and support which I thus get to my back and hips during a severe run with the hounds is most beneficial.

I sometimes use shoulder straps, which at school were always drawn very tight. The management of our corsets was handed over to the two ladies who assisted their father in the instruction of the pupils. Every morning we were inspected by the fair disciplinarians before they gave us a long drilling lesson.

On such occasions our corsets were expected to be laced an inch tighter than during the rest of the day, except when we had dancing lessons twice a week in the afternoon.

I know perfectly well that some people will cry out against such constraint enforced on growing lads. But experience has taught me to look back with gratitude on a system which made me feel I could not slouch about in the manner which is far too usual in the case of boys in the present day.

The first week or two the younger lady, in the absence of her sister, took the drilling herself, and I found it at first very difficult tightly laced as I was, to go through the movements required of me. However, the lady was soon able to remedy my awkward efforts, though I am afraid at the time I thought her ill-natured in the sharp stimulants now and then applied to my ankles by her little stinging whip, or across my cheeks from her dainty kid-gloved palm.

I am confident that no exercise ever did me such good as those drilling lessons gone through in a strong, firmly-laced corset. I can only say that during the whole time I was at that school my lace was never permitted to be put aside, indeed the last month the younger sister ordered me sleep in my corset, a restraint which I must say I disliked exceedingly.

I must confess I do not approve of such restraint at night, and the treatment was very exceptional. In my case I deserved it for disobedience.

I am sure the subject of corset-wearing is one of great interest, and I trust to read the experiences of some of your correspondents in reference to it. I shall be glad if you can find space for my long letter.–Yours faithfully, V.S.

'Curb' and others continued the correspondence.

4 February 1893, p. 363.

I am glad to notice from the appearance of the letter of 'V.S.' that you are again printing letters on the important question of the corset and its kindred appliances for disciplinary purposes. No doubt some persons will consider that 'V.S.' was hardly used in having his efforts stimulated in the way he mentions; but for my part, I do not think so at all, as I am one of the very strongest believers in the advantages to be derived by a lad from a spell of the improving discipline which he can alone receive from a strict ruler chosen from the fair sex. However imperious the lady may be–and from personal experience under the ladies I have mentioned in former letters, I know that that may

No. 7.—DRESS FOR BOY OF
SIX OR SEVEN YEARS OF AGE.

No. 8.—WALKING-DRESS
FOR LITTLE GIRL.

16.   (a) Dress for Boy of Six or Seven Years of Age.   (b) Walking-Dress for Little Girl.
The Young Ladies' Journal, 1876, vol. 13, p.504.

mean a good deal–he should be required to submit, and he cannot help but benefit. It is simply marvellous the improvement which a smart girl of resolute will can force in the most clumsy and unwilling of pupils. I know, and readers of my last letter will readily understand, that I was a most unpromising subject, yet under the persuasive influence brought to bear upon me, I soon learned obedience and improved in manners, as well as learning my schoolwork twice as well as ever I had done before. As to learning to dance I never should have done so, and so far from walking properly or standing upright I should have continued to slouch to the end of my days. But I did learn to dance, and I did learn to walk and stand in the manner required of me. There was no choice in the matter, whatever was commanded had to be obeyed. No word of objection was permitted for a single instant, and it was useless to hope for carelessness to pass unnoticed, or, if one was foolish enough to do so, he was speedily undeceived with a sharpness that, as a rule, prevented his erring in the same way again for some time. Your last correspondent appears to have found his chief trouble arise from the difficulties put in his way by the unaccustomed restraint of his corset. Although I certainly found this irksome at first, the greatest source of misfortune to me was the elevation of my heels. At first I was for ever turning my foot, or stumbling, or dragging my heel on the ground with a gritty noise, or else failing to stand as required with knees well back, and being found instead in a cab-horse kind of attitude. Now this was not wilful on my part, but simply arose from my native clumsiness, and the difficulty I found in adapting myself to the smart, but unaccustomed, footgear I was required to wear. There was no gradual raising of the heels in my case, but at the particular request of the lady who introduced me, Madame had put me at once into the chaussure of one who had reached the higher ranks, whilst her daughters had to teach me as best they could, and the natural consequence was that they spared no pains to force me up to the level at which I was supposed to be placed; and many a time I have received slash after slash with the whip, which applied upon a foot protected by only the very thinnest of stockings, and the very tightest of thin kid boots, stung terribly, when really I was trying my best. This was undeniably very sharp discipline, yet I certainly benefited by it, and I cannot blame the young ladies for using their powers to make me keep up to the high level at which they were expected to keep the class, though I cannot pretend that they hesitated a moment between stinging me and incurring the least risk of blame themselves for my clumsiness. Under this discipline I progressed in a manner which no other means would have accomplished, and it is just in this way that a pretty martinet has such an enormous advantage in dealing with a youth when both know that however exacting she may be he must submit. I trust that your correspondent ['D.S.' 21 May 1892] who some time since asked me for information will not discourage his governess by putting restrictions in her way, or depriving her of the great power which a riding whip to be used at her free will affords her. She is probably already aware that the more tightly a pretty hand is gloved the more stinging a slap it can give. Many a time have my cheeks tingled under the application of the most innocent-looking little hand in delicate kid that fitted so tightly that I had just found no little trouble in buttoning it. But the most painful punishment of all was the slashing with the whip across our own hands when protected only by thin tight kid. This last punishment was especially used whenever we soiled the pale kid gloves we were required to wear on dancing days, and which, no matter what we had to do, we were expected to keep perfectly clean, a requirement which our rulers well knew, though we were in those days nominally at liberty, except when dancing or at drill, in reality kept us under very tight restraint.–
Yours, etc., CURB

On 18 February 1893 (pp. 394-5), 'A Confirmed Tight Lacer' wrote in favour of tight-lacing for men. Of his childhood he said: 'Being myself a delicate lad, always under the doctor,

94

my mother, with the view of improving my health, put me at twelve years of age into strong, well-boned stays, with a stout, wooden busk, shoulder straps, and lacing behind, and laced me up as tightly as I could bear. I well remember the discomfort that for some time I had to endure, but what has been the result? I have worn similarly-made corsets (although I am married and a family man) for the last fifty years; first, because from my putting them on my health steadily improved, and for a long time has been as good almost as it could be; and secondly, because I have found them thoroughly comfortable.' The mother of the next correspondent seems to have found her son of an awkward rather than of an unhealthy nature.

TIGHT LACING   11 March 1993, p. 26.
Having worn stays for the last seven years my experience may interest some of your readers. I was a rough, awkward boy of sixteen when my mother called me into her room one day, and, showing me a pair of stays, told me I was to wear them. No notice was taken of my objections, and I was soon laced into them quite tightly enough to prevent me from bending as the stays were of the most extreme stiffness, and my discomfort was not lessened by the tight fastenings of a pair of shoulder straps which kept me perfectly upright. From that day no relaxation was permitted me, every morning a maid drew my stays as tight as possible, so that I went about to my lessons and play every day more closely laced in with a smaller waist and stiffer gait than most girls. In a few months I became quite reconciled to the restraint, and soon grew to like the feeling of being tightly laced in my long strong stays which kept me always upright, and prevented any awkward movements. I have never relinquished the practice since, my health has never suffered, and the warmth and comfort I enjoy is very great. Yours truly,   A BELIEVER IN STAYS

This letter met with the approval of 'A Confirmed Tight-Lacer,' who wrote on 22 April 1893 (pp. 123-4): 'I am glad to see in your valuable paper another unequivocal testimony in favour of tight-lacing from a stay-wearer of seven years, converted against his will by the stronger will of a sensible mother, who, convinced that it would be for her lad's good that he should be thoroughly well-laced, put him at sixteen into good stout stays, and from that day, notwithstanding all the young gentleman's protestations, laced him up as tightly as he could bear.' The writer then summarised the latter half of the previous letter and also quoted most of Walter's letter from *E.D.M.* of November 1867. He expressed the view that it would 'conduce much to both the health and the good manners of our young people if both boys and girls at the age of twelve were put into properly-fitted stout stays, and were alike well-laced'. On 13 May 1893 the paper printed two more letters from men who had experienced the corset at school, one in Vienna.

TIGHT LACING   13 May 1893, p. 172.
The correspondence on this subject is very interesting, and I hope you can find room for a few words from one who has had some experience in the matter. I was, as a lad, a most unpromising subject for improvement of the figure, as up to the age of sixteen I was allowed by my guardian unrestrained licence to eat what was on the table, and to slouch about bent almost double. When I was that age my guardian sent me to a school where great attention was paid to the figure. No sentimental idea of pampering the lads was indulged in, but I and the thirty other lads, most of whom were as old as I was, and some two years older, were obliged to wear strong, stout corsets, which were laced each morning as firmly as possible by two maids when we came down to be inspected before breakfast by our principal's wife, who herself had had the great advantage of going through the *régime* of an extremely fashionable finishing school in Paris. As you are also allowing a correspondence on gloves and the care of the hands, I may be permitted to state that I never saw such exquisitely lovely hands as those of

this young lady. She nearly always wore dainty thin kid gloves. I hope to hear more on this important subject. Yours faithfully, STAYS

13 May 1893, p. 172.
Being home for a holiday from my school in Vienna, and having read your correspondence, it may interest your readers to know that the majority of boys and men there wear corsets as a regular article of dress. When I arrived about three years ago, aged thirteen, a corset was selected, and, in spite of my rebellion, clasped on me; then the lacing commenced, and I soon began to feel that my old freedom of movement was leaving me, for, as the lace was tightened, the long, strong corset held me more and more erect, and when the lace was tied and the shoulder straps were tightly buckled (both out of my reach), I found myself thoroughly under stay-lace *régime*. Stooping or lolling about was out of the question, for I was kept rigidly stiff and upright all day. It was very uncomfortable at first, but by the next morning, when we were all laced up, I was more reconciled to the restraint, and by degrees became a willing subject to the strongly-boned corset in which my figure was always confined.

My school fellows take a great pride in being well-corseted; the new boys are soon anxious to be laced as tightly as possible, and I myself feel quite uncomfortable if my long, snug-fitting corset is not drawn in close and tight, keeping my waist at its usual size of 18-ins. Yours obediently, AN UPRIGHT FIGURE
North Kensington, W.

In the course of a letter mainly about ladies' boots and shoes, 'Admirer of Pretty Feet' included this paragraph about ladies disciplining boys:

10 June 1893, pp. 235-6.
A propos des bottes. I think some of those who are against the exercise of discipline by ladies over youths would do well to consider the principle involved of submission on account of duty instead of mere brute force. A correspondent this week puts this in plain words [not identified], as I did when writing you on the subject some years ago [8 June 1889 and 25 January 1890], and I think a proper appreciation of this would stop a lot of unreasoning fuss. Of course, in some cases, the discipline is more stringent than in others, but I have never known the least harm done. There is never the same sense of oppression and sullen resentment where the discipline–even if sharp, and even perhaps, a trifle tyrannical–is experienced at the hands of a pretty woman as there is under the bullying of a pedagogue. The pupil soon learns to yield to authority instead of merely to weight and violence, so that the best results are achieved.

AN ADMIRER OF PRETTY FEET

'Marielle', who claimed to be a school mistress and wrote about corsets and high heels, complimented 'Admirer' on the foregoing in the final paragraph of a letter on 'Figure Training'. She also approved of corset discipline.

5 August 1893, p. 364.
I was greatly pleased to see the letter a week or two ago of 'Admirer of Pretty Feet' so strongly emphasising tightness and pointed shape as elements of prettiness in a promenade boot. I should think 'Curb', too, would hold pretty strong views on this subject. Gentlemen who have been under the *régime* called by your correspondents 'Corset Discipline', are generally most ardent admirers. Since I have been led to refer to the subject, I would like to say that, whilst I have the greatest objection to stay-wearing or high-heeled men as a general rule, I considered the discipline *régime* an extremely good plan for driving the awkwardness out of hobbledehoys. MARIELLE.

In a letter about 'Tight Lacing for Men', E. MacEwan of Paisley pointed out that victims of corset discipline might enjoy it.

19 August 1893, p. 396.
Some correspondents seem to discredit the letters on corset discipline which have appeared in this column, chiefly because of the resistance which they suppose a boy could make while being laced up, forgetting that he might be as desirous of lacing as his mistress would be to lace him. When a boy myself, I was passionately fond of small waists, and would gladly have submitted to the course of figure training described by 'White Cat', who got her nephew into tight, stiff stays, and kept him in them by means of a locked steel belt. One day I discovered a pair of disused corsets of small size, which I secretly appropriated, and soon thereafter experienced the delightful sensations of tight-lacing. With these corsets I often laced myself to a size which many ladies would deem very small. And even yet, though 5ft. 10in. in height, I can get into 20in. and believe I should enjoy the life of your correspondent 'Caradoc', could I but come within the influence of a lady like his wife, who regularly laces him into well-nigh inflexible corset, and meets all his objections with an extra application of the lace. . . .

E. MACEWAN.

'V.S.' wrote on 7 January 1893 about his experiences at an Austrian school. On 26 August 1893 this item was included in 'Questions'. Obviously 'V.S.' was seeking a personal correspondent: 'Will anyone in London experienced in corset discipline, undertake or advise the wearing of corsets by a young gentleman engaged in sedentary occupation during the day. Address with Editor.–"V.S."' Towards the end of 1893 three new correspondents, 'Corset', 'Alice' and 'A Slim Waisted Maid', described the treatment of boys who wore stays. Punishment or discipline is not directly involved, but there is an emphasis on enforced girlishness.

A VICTIM OF FIGURE TRAINING   30 September 1893, p. 76.
I came across a case of a boy being kept very tightly laced, which may interest your readers. A lady here had twins. When they reached eleven years of age the girl died, so she determined to bring up the boy with all the care she had lavished on the girl. He is a pretty child, with fair curls, a delicate pale complexion, a neat shape–though inclined to stoutness, which in spite of careful dieting, a fair amount of walking exercise, and the constant restraint of tight stays, is gradually getting a pronounced embonpoint below the waist. This is a constant annoyance to his mother, who tries by every means of supporting belt and semi-starvation to reduce the size of his figure at this point. He has a remarkably feminine appearance, which was much remarked on by the people who had tea with his mother a few days ago. She quite dotes on this, her only child, and hopes he will one day be a great artist, for which art he has great aptitude, though he is never to be allowed to go to school, his mother being afraid of the contact of rough school boys. He came down to tea, dressed in black velvet knickerbockers and jacket with broad soft collar. The jacket was cut tight to his figure, and confined at the waist by a metal belt, which showed off his wonderfully slender waist and well-laced figure in a perfect fitting corset. The three fashionable young ladies present were surprised, and far from pleased, to find on measurement their waists were all nearly two inches bigger than that of the plump, picturesque boy with long, silky curls, pale fair complexion, and small girlish hands. He is always dressed in the morning in an exquisitely moulded corset, that preserves his tiny wasp waist to its usual size, in spite of the plump proportions of his shoulders, arms and neck. His hands will never lose their pretty shape and colour, night gloves being part of his dress, besides well-fitting long dogskin, worn a large part of the day, partly to keep his hands small and delicate, and also to preserve their whiteness. Unless I am much mistaken, his delicate clear

skin is not only indebted to his pinched figure and the pain inflicted by his stays, but also to the use of cosmetics by his mother when she sees him off to bed. It is extraordinary that his mother does not see what a bad effect on his health her extreme system of lacing is producing.

Grand Hotel, Glasgow. CORSET.

Meanwhile 'Curb' replied to 'Marielle'. He expressed his agreement with her about the style of ladies' boots, but had this to say about the comment quoted above.

30 September 1893, p. 76.

I wonder whether when 'Marielle' lightly remarks on the excellence of 'the discipline *régime*' for 'driving the awkwardness out of hobbledehoys', she has any idea of the bad quarters of an hour (or good deal more) sometimes spent by the 'hobbledehoys' in the process. To take a lad without the slightest warning from his rough freedom, and lace him up in a tight long-waisted corset, boned and steeled to the stiffest, strap back his shoulders, case his hands and wrists in long, tight white kid gloves, which he is required to keep perfectly fresh and unsoiled (a requirement entailing wondrous care), fix up his chin so that he cannot see his toes, and without any previous training, put him on boots of extreme pointed shape and tightness, perched upon heels of tip-toe height and the most tapering form. To do this, and then straightway punish him for every fault as though he had had the advantage of long training, and stimulate his efforts with the sharpest application of a stinging whip at the slightest falter, is a proceeding which, however beneficial, is hardly the plan which the subject of it would voluntarily select for himself. CURB.

A REMARKABLE STORY OF TIGHT-LACING 7 October 1893, p. 92.

I never was quite able to credit 'White Cat's' story of how she compelled a boy of fifteen to wear stays and obey her in the most slavish manner [13 September 1890], but I lately came across a case of somewhat the same nature.

I was in a country village for a holiday, where I made the acquaintance of an elderly maiden lady and her nephew. After the acquaintance had ripened, and we knew more of each other, the lady told me that she adopted the boy when he was about seven, that she found him a docile, quiet little fellow, and she, having a great objection to men through early disappointment, determined to bring him up at home, never to allow him to go to school, and to make more of a girl of him than a boy.

She dressed him in stays, but with a blouse and knickerbockers, not petticoats–and when he was a little over twelve she began to tighten his stays gradually. She had always laced rather tightly, and now, to encourage him to obtain a small waist, she used to make him lace her stays very tightly every day as she did his. In this way he began to take an interest in it, for he was devoted to his aunt, and to please her he used to tighten his stays even more than she ordered. By the time he was fifteen he had a figure like a girl, and, as he never went to school or associated with other boys, he was not afraid of ridicule, but was quite proud of his waist. He generally wore a loose blouse with a belt, but for evening wear he had a velvet jacket, open in front to show shirt and waistcoat, but shaped to the back quite tightly so as to show off the figure, of which the aunt was as proud as the boy–the white or black velvet waistcoat fitted accurately. Black velvet breeches, with black silk stockings and high-heeled patent leather shoes and lavender-coloured kid gloves completed his evening costume. When I first saw him in this attire, and with his light brown hair curled over his head and forehead, I thought he was a girl. His aunt had taught him to do needlework and wait upon her like a lady's maid. She had him taught to dress lady's hair by a coiffeur, and I noticed that her hair was most fashionably dressed and curled; she told me he was the best maid she ever had.

This eccentric lady is very rich and can amply provide for the boy, otherwise it would have been a very wicked thing to do, for, of course, the boy is utterly ruined for any manly occupation. He is musical, and plays fairly-well on the piano and guitar. He is too tightly laced to play lawn tennis or take any exercise beyond a gentle walk, nor can he sing, and I have never seen a good singer who was tight laced. He goes to bed every night with his hair in curl-papers, but does not sleep in stays. His aunt considers that quite unnecessary, and certainly aunt and nephew have very small waists without resorting to that plan. She told me she has his stays made for him by her London *corsetière*, who comes down on purpose to measure and fit him and her every six months. The stays are always of satin and trimmed with lace. She told him to bring me a pair to look at, and he fetched a beautiful little corset 17 in. in the waist, of very delicate pale pink satin. He has them of all light colours–the aunt considers black satin to be bourgeois, and will not let him wear them, but always white or quite light colour. They are made exactly the same as ladies' stays, only without the fullness of the bust, well steeled and boned, with a straight busk and silk lace.

It is really a very curious case, and, I think, may interest some of your readers. He is in fair health, but looks delicate. Yours faithfully, ALICE

Kensington, Sept. 23, 1893.

In the 'Questions' column of 14 October 1893 (p. 108) Patience Gregory asked: ' Will "Alice" of Kensington kindly inform me whether this boy's ears were pierced by his aunt to wear gold sleepers therein ?'

On 12 August and 9 September 1893, a new contributor, A. Williams, wrote about tight-lacing in the Russian Army at the time of the Napoleonic wars. In the second of those letters he mentioned that there was a book in his father's library 'in which life in the barracks, and at the Cadet College at Moscow or St. Petersburg, is described. I forget the details but there is a long description of the waist tightening that was practised there early in the present century.' He promised to translate the relevant chapter. He now keeps his promise.

MILITARY TIGHT-LACING IN RUSSIA   28 October 1893, p. 140.

As I promised in a previous letter, I have translated the following account of the lacing practised in the Russian Military College at Moscow in 1800. The author, Tschikagow, in describing his life as a cadet, states: 'My body was then compressed in a long corset of a strong cotton material full of bones, which had been made for me on arrival at the college. We stood in a row, and each hooked together the front of his corset, and we were then, in succession, laced up till the corsets met behind. The corsets came nearly up to our armpits, and lessened our waists by about one-fourth of their circumference. Our young bones at fourteen years of age offered but a poor resistance to the practised skill of the corset makers, who drew us in with a rapidity that made us breathless, and then knotted the lace. The tailors then measured us for our uniforms, which fitted over the corsets with extreme tightness. Our civilian costume was then sent to our homes, so that from that time we could not wear anything but our uniform, and that only by the aid of the stays. We laced each other up in the morning, and severe was the punishment we received if our uniforms were strained by an insufficiently-laced corset. We felt little pain at our outdoor work, but sitting at our desks numbed and scored our young bodies terribly. The senior cadets delighted to inflict on us all the rigors [*sic*] they had themselves endured, and punished any breach of cadet etiquette by lacing us in very small corsets they termed the "tormentors". Once these were fastened they were kept unloosed for days, when they well earned their name of "tormentors".'

Further on the author describes two years later, when the vanity of young men led to extraordinary extravagance, but of this more anon.–Yours truly, A. WILLIAMS.

NO. 1.—SUIT FOR LITTLE BOY FROM FIVE TO EIGHT YEARS OF AGE.

NO. 2.—HOME-DRESS FOR LITTLE GIRL FROM SIX TO EIGHT YEARS OF AGE.

NO.

17. (a) Suit for Little Boy from Five to Eight Years of Age.
     (b) Home-Dress for Little Girl from Six to Eight Years of Age.

The Young Ladies' Journal, 1878, vol. 15, p. 488.

The third report of a tight-laced boy was supplied by 'A Slim Waisted Maid'.

TIGHT-LACING EXTRAORDINARY   25 November 1893, p. 204.
Having read some letters in your paper by 'Corset' and 'Alice', and having some experience in the subject, it may interest your readers to know that the cases spoken of are by no means rare. I am maid to a lady who has an only child, a boy of fourteen, and she is very particular about his appearance. He always wears stays, and they are very long and beautifully shaped and as stiff as whalebone can make them. In the morning I have to lace him up quite tightly, and strap back his shoulders, and at eleven o'clock I lace his stays close and put him on a pair of long tight kid gloves, which he wears all day to keep his hands soft and white. His waist is now nineteen inches, which he finds fairly comfortable, although the corseting is so effective that he cannot possibly stoop, and of course, romping about is quite out of the question.
On Sundays, and for parties, he wears his best pair of stays, which are extra long and have a stiff steel busk. When they are close he has a slim round waist of seventeen and a half inches and as good a figure as a tight-laced girl. His shoulders are then well strapped back, so that he is obliged to keep quite upright. For parties his hands are gloved in white kid of the tightest possible fit, and with his feet in tight, high-heeled shoes he looks very pretty and graceful, and dances beautifully. This training does not affect his health in the least and he is quite reconciled to the restraint and perfectly happy in submitting to it.
I think if all boys were made to wear stays they would be very much improved in manners and appearance. They would become accustomed to the restraint, as girls do, and would then submit (as all girls have to do who wish to look nice) to the slight inconveniences of tight lacing. At my mistress's wish, I always lace as tight as possible myself, and am quite proud to call myself,   A SLIM WAISTED MAID

Earrings for boys and men were much discussed in *The Family Doctor*, but so far I have not included any letters on the subject. The following is an exception because the boy's aunt was hostile to boys and seems to have had the boy's ears pierced deliberately as a feminine adornment.

EARRINGS   20 January 1894, pp. 330-1.
I was much interested in the letter of 'A Lazy Man' [He seems to mean 'Idle Man' of 9 December 1893.], and should very much like to know how the holes in the tops and sides of his ears were bored, and what kind of rings he wears in them. Did he do them himself, or a jeweller? Several lady correspondents have described having holes bored in the tops and sides of their ears, but 'A Lazy Man' is the first of the other sex who has been so operated upon. As to the pleasure to be derived from wearing rings in the holes of the ears, I can speak from experience, for I have worn them for a long time. As a boy, I was brought up by an aunt in the country, and disliking rough boys, she decided to bring me up more as a girl. Up to the age of eight I was dressed as a girl, but after that I assumed boys' clothes, though for some years I was more effeminately dressed than most boys. When I was about six years old my aunt decided to have my ears pierced, not on account of any benefit to the eyes, but simply because she wished me to wear earrings, of which ornaments she herself was very fond. At first I objected and begged her not to have my ears bored, but she insisted, and took me to a jeweller (a lady), who in spite of my objections, soon had the earrings in my ear holes. The operation was quite painless, though, child-like, I was very much frightened at it beforehand. I wore small gold sleepers for about three months, when my aunt removed them and put into my ears instead, a pair of very small gold and coral eardrops, which I wore continuously (night and day) till I was put into boys' clothes. I then

resumed the sleepers, but I missed my ear-drops very much, as I had grown to like the feeling of them dangling in my ears. At my own request my aunt allowed me to wear them in the house, but later on she got me a small gold hoops, anchor pattern, which I wore constantly till I left the country and came to London. I was very fond of my ear-rings and wore them in spite of some ridicule I got at school for them. One or two of my school fellows wished to follow my example, and one boy, after much trouble, per-suaded his mother to allow him to have his ears bored and wear gold sleepers. The parents of the others refused. After I came to London, I gave up wearing earrings in public, but always wear them at home. I generally wear a pair of large ear-drops as I like to feel I have something in my ears. I often thank my aunt for insisting on piercing my ears, and not giving way to my tears, and I have no intention of giving up wearing earrings.   MALE-EARRINGS

The last two letters from *The Family Doctor* are both relevant to the theme of 'Military Tight-Lacing.'

TIGHT LACING   3 February 1894, p. 362.
     As your correspondents still appear interested in the subject of stays, it will prob-ably not surprise them that the wearing of corsets is a fashion that seems to spread more and more abroad. I have heard of tight-lacing being enforced in English schools, but have never met anyone who has personally undergone the treatment. This year it is very noticeable that much younger children, both English, colonial and foreign are made to undergo the discipline of the lace, evidently to ensure extreme slenderness of waist as early as possible. Two children, of ten and thirteen, staying at Mentone, have their figures encased in old-fashioned bodices, coming high enough up to allow of their arms passing through holes; the fronts are quite stiff, and very long and pointed. The elder especially is laced up so tightly that people always stop and stare after the slim figure, buttoned up tightly in a perfect-fitting jacket, the waist so extremely pinched and waspish that people wonder how the child can bear to walk; the stomacher front also making her as straight and stiff as a dart. Both children have bad complexions, sal-low and unhealthy, which is not to be wondered at; but their faces are amply compen-sated for, in their mother's opinion, by their really lovely hair, of which they have mas-ses, and the whiteness of their hands, which are models of shape and colour. Their mother, a handsome Dutch lady, told me she first put a belt round her girls as early as five years old, drawing it tighter till they were eight, when regular stiff corsets were substituted. She showed me a photo of her husband when a boy at a Russian cadet col-lege. It represented a remarkably handsome youth, with a figure as slim and tightly laced as a female beauty; he was a great pet amongst fashionable ladies, especially on account of his waist, which by a very severe system of lacing never exceeded in size that of the reigning star in the theatrical world. He was made to go through the long and very arduous gymnastic classes, with his figure always as strictly confined as when but-toned up on parade or in a lady's drawing room. His health failed from the constant strain of violent exercise, which was developing his chest, though his waist was still confined to the most girlish size. His relations and the military authorities refused to allow him to loosen his waist, and even made him lace tighter to counteract his growing weight; he soon became a constant visitor to the hospital, and was at length sent home as too weak to make a soldier. He is now a martyr to his congested liver, and will prob-ably never regain his health, though still a handsome, upright man. There are twins who attend a dancing class here; they are about ten or eleven years old. By a whim of the mother they are dressed exactly alike–large knickerbockers, velvet doublets, cut to fit the figure closely, and show off slim, well-corseted waists; broad lace collars, and the hair long and falling to the waist. Both children have equally white, well kept

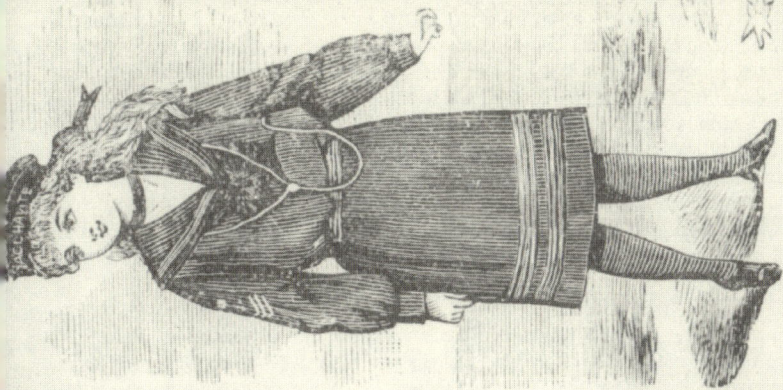

MAN O' WAR

SUITS FOR BOYS & GIRLS.

JOHN REDFERN & SONS beg to call the attention of ladies to the above children's tailor-made garments, which they have supplied to nearly all the Royal and Imperial Courts of Europe.

These suits, made from strong English Serges, carefully selected and shrunk, are guaranteed to wear well, and to retain their colour to the last.

Patterns, Sketches, Measurement forms, and all Particulars sent, on application to

REDFERN,

COWES, ISLE OF WIGHT.

18. Man o' War Suits for Boys and Girls.   *Lady's Pictorial*, 15 May 1886 (following p. 448).

hands, waists the same size, and neat feet, in high-heeled shoes; so no one but their own mother can tell the girl from the boy. Some years hence the boy will be sent to a military academy in Austria, somewhat like the one described by your correspondent under the heading of 'Military Tight-lacing'; his slim ballet-girl figure will be well prepared for the compression it will probably be subjected to. In conclusion, I may say that, in my opinion, should a very slim waist be considered more essential for a girl than complexion, robustness, and strong health, the wearing of stays can hardly be begun too early, as the bones are easily compressed in a child of eight or ten, and she has become accustomed to the restraint by the time that many mothers begin the really severe lacing, continued night and day, necessary to secure the veritable tiny wasp waist of the *débutante* of eighteen summers.–Yours, etc., R.E.B.
Grand Hotel, Nice.

MILITARY TIGHT-LACING 24 February 1894, p. 410.
I must apologise for the long delay in continuing the translations on this subject. There are further references to this subject further on in the book, which are as follows, as nearly as I can translate them: 'At fifteen, or sixteen, a change came over our feelings towards our hitherto hated corsets. About this age we went out into society a great deal during our holidays, and finding the admiration of the ladies a novel and attractive delight, and, further finding that our slender waists came in for a large share of admiration, a rage for tight-lacing set in among us. The ladies at that time followed this fashion, and, as each cadet had some special divinity at whose shrine he worshipped, a rivalry regarding waists arose between many ladies and their attendant cadets. Many of the cadets laced to such an extent that it seriously impeded their studies. They would, with each other's assistance, or as was more often the case, by the assistance of certain corset makers, draw themselves in to incredibly small dimensions. The ladies, jealous at this, would playfully insist that the prerogative of slenderness rested with them, and further rivalries would ensue. The cadets would resolutely resist any attempt to outdo them, and in these endeavours their waists were still further reduced. Corsets were not taken off at night, but were still further tightened, and as time went on and the cadets joined the army the habit of lacing became firmly rooted in them.' Then follows a number of figures relating to the sizes of waists, which I will leave till another day, should your readers care to hear more on this subject. Yours truly,
A. WILLIAMS

Either A. Williams did not write again, or his letter was not published. In any case his was the last of the letters about boys or men wearing stays. Two letters on male cross dressing were printed in June 1894 and are included in *Men in Petticoats*. The paper in effect closed the correspondence with two serious articles on 'Corsets in Relation to Health' on 14 and 28 July 1894. Two or three more letters appeared on 'tight-lacing', the last on 5 April 1895. The paper ceased publication in 1918 and I do not believe that there are any similar letters in that intervening period.

v.   The Fashions.

The Englishwoman's Domestic Magazine, May 1867.

Journal des Demoiselles, May 1873.

VI

ANSWERS

Alfred Harmsworth, later Viscount Northcliffe, published the first number of the weekly *Answers To Correspondents*, soon renamed simply *Answers*, on 2 June 1888. It was modelled on the pattern of *Tit-Bits* founded by George Newnes on 22 October 1881. Correspondence from readers was naturally encouraged and tight-lacing soon came up for discussion. I reproduce two letters where men wore stays in their youth, the first, like 'Walter' of *The Englishwoman's Domestic Magazine*, 1867, at an Austrian school.

WHERE MEN WEAR STAYS   20 April 1889, p. 333.
    I am much interested in the subject of small waists, which is open to discussion in your paper.
    I am a warm admirer of a slender waist, which is a great addition to the charms of the fair sex.
    I remember in Austria, where I resided for some years, what perfect figures the women possessed. And there the corset is drawn much tighter than it usually is with us.
    Tight-lacing, in many parts of the Continent, is by no means confined to members of the gentler sex.
    All the officers in Vienna and the majority of the better-class civilians lace up by no means loosely, and look smart and trim.
    At the age of sixteen I was sent to a school kept by a retired officer of the Austrian army.
    All his pupils were required to wear stays, and though I, as an English boy, was very indignant at first, I never suffered any harm from the use of corsets, and a smarter set of lads it would have been difficult to find.
    We were forced to hold ourselves well up, and the strong corset prevented slouching.
    I shall never forget the lovely figures of our principal's two daughters.
    I never saw in England anything approaching the slim waists of those two continental beauties who used to vie with each other as to who could have the slenderest waist and the daintiest gloved hands.
    They had exquisitely delicate soft white hands, which, as a boy, I had reason to look on with more dread than admiration, for the young ladies helped their father in the tuition of his pupils, and woe betide the unlucky boy who displeased either of the pretty martinets.
    My face seems to tingle even now when I think of their pretty kid-gloved hands; they always put on a pair of gloves before punishing us to save their soft taper fingers from tingling against our ears. But to come back more nearly to the subject of small waists. I simply beg to suggest that if young ladies can lace tight without any practical inconvenience, pray let them do so, and so gratify the eyes of those who like to see a trim figure.
    I am, yours faithfully,   STAYS.

    P.S. I forgot to mention that the two young ladies looked the picture of health, and had the most brilliant complexions.

MALE CORSET WEARERS

25 November 1893, p. 13.

From the 'Confessions of a Male Corset Wearer' one would be led to suppose that corset-wearing by men is very unusual, but I think that it is not nearly so uncommon as one would suppose.

I understand that the officers in most of our crack cavalry regiments wear stays, as a matter of course, as they find it impossible to wear their tight uniforms with either comfort or smartness otherwise.

I was brought up by an aunt who kept a ladies' school in the South of England, and the old lady made me wear tight stays, as she said they would make me grow straight and give me a good figure. So I was laced every morning regularly until I was eighteen, when I left her charge to go into business.

At first I was rather bashful about ordering stays for myself, but the staymaker lady to whom I went told me I need not trouble myself on that point, as she had several gentlemen clients for whom she worked regularly, and I myself know several men who always wear corsets, but none so insane as to lace so tight that he cannot go up or down stairs naturally.

A moderately tight stay is very comfortable to wear, and makes the coat fit much better. Yours,

London W.C.

LACE.

VII

MODERN SOCIETY

Modern Society began publication as a weekly 'society' paper on 4 December 1880, but copies of the paper are not available in the British Newspaper Library until 25 November 1882. As a typical 'society' paper it specialised in gossip and news of royalty, the aristocracy and the upper classes. This was set out in a long series of miscellaneous paragraphs in the first part of the paper. There were also reviews of the Arts, Theatre and Music and articles on fashion. There was no regular correspondence column as such, but letters from readers on a variety of subjects were inserted in the main run of society paragraphs. The wearing of stays by men and women recurred as a subject every so often. I include those letters where boys were made to wear corsets for one reason or another. 'Forty Years a Male Stay-Wearer' was made to wear them at a school, a French school.

17 August 1889, p. 1018.

Early left an orphan I was sent to a French boarding school. The morning after my arrival my figure was carefully measured. Two days later the principal sent for me, and I found a corset maker there with some pairs of stays. One of these, to my great surprise she proceeded, despite my protestations, to lace me into, and I was then informed that it was the headmaster's rule that everyone in the house without distinction of sex, should wear stays, he and his sons being no exception. At first I found the restriction irksome, but other English boys assured me that they had very soon become accustomed to it and were then not only reconciled but felt the even pressure of the waist and the support given to the figure truly delightful.

In the case of each boy, exact instructions were given as to the reduction of his waist from time to time. Every morning when we were getting up, a master and a maid servant came in; the former superintended, while the latter laced our stays. These were well boned, and had an individual busk, laced behind. Though I was a broad shouldered fellow, my waist ultimately measured eighteen inches. Notwithstanding our stays we were as jolly as other boys and quite as well, and how much better we looked than boys who lounged about with bent backs!

My own sons, as soon as they were twelve years of age, had to submit to the discipline of the corset, and I can assure you that with their slender waists (for their waistcoats were close fitting to show off their figures), their splendid carriage, and scotch kilts, they were the handsomest boys in town. Let me assure men who have never worn stays that they do not know what an immense comfort they are.

FORTY YEARS A MALE STAY-WEARER

In a letter protesting against excessive tight lacing, 'another correspondent' included this remark about boys.

13 April 1895, p. 688.

I personally know, even in enlightened Edinburgh, several cases where tight-lacing is practised to an almost barbarous extent, and the 'locked corset' you mentioned a few weeks ago in your paper is in constant use. Absurd though it may seem, I know two or three families where the boys are made to wear well-laced stiff corsets–their mothers telling me they thought 'it vastly improved their boys' figures and carriage'. Can this fashionable folly go much further than this?

Some mothers thought stays beneficial for health. A correspondent from Bournemouth on 10 July 1897 (p. 1107) said that when he was a boy he suffered very much from a weak back, 'and my mother, following the doctor's advice, made me wear corsets. I am thankful to say that I have now quite recovered, but find corsets so comfortable that I always wear them'. 'Acton' was put into stays at the whim of his aunt.

20 August 1898, p. 1296.

Perhaps some of your readers would like to hear the experience of a member of the male sex who knows something of tight lacing. When I was a boy of thirteen, I came under the care of a rich, but eccentric maiden aunt, who in spite of my remonstrances, insisted on my wearing stays. I was taken to a first-class Parisian *corsetière* and measured for a pair of 23in. satin corsets, the natural size of my waist being twenty-five inches. So exquisitely did these fit, that though I wore them continuously night and day, to my surprise I found from the first that the sensation of wearing well-boned, firmly-laced stays was an extremely delightful one. At the end of every month I was fitted into a new pair of corsets exactly a quarter of an inch smaller in the waist than the previous pair, until in two and a half years, when I was fifteen and a half years old, my waist only measured sixteen inches. I never felt the slightest discomfort or suffered at all in health, owing, no doubt, to the gradual way in which my figure was trained, and I always derived great pleasure from the feeling of my tightly-laced corsets.

ACTON

There was a batch of these letters in July 1899. As a boy 'R.B.' tried on corsets for fun, enjoyed it, but gave it up for health reasons. 'Martyr', however, was the victim of an aunt who hated boys and wished to make him girlish, even dressing him as one in the evenings. 'Tamed' was taken into a ladies' shop by his stepmother and fitted out with stays, just like the youth trained by 'White Cat' in *The Family Doctor* of 13 September 1890. 'Trained in Time' claimed that the boys in her family always wore stays, while 'Malta' was put into stays at a German school.

8 July 1899, p. 1105.

My parents were fashionable corset-makers, and when I was a small boy, I had frequent opportunities of trying on corsets of all kinds, and knew that even tightly-laced stays were by no means the hardship they are generally said to be. In two or three years I began to suffer much from indigestion, and upon the urgent advice of my doctor, reluctantly gave up my satin 'armour'. There is no doubt that all who have tried it agree that the sensation of wearing firmly laced corsets is pleasant, and that when not too tight they are not harmful; but as one gets used to them there is an inevitable tendency to lace them more and more tightly, and to have them still more stiffly boned. The digestion is then, as in my case, sure to suffer, and on this account, and also the amount of ridicule they must incur, I think no sensible mother will make her boys wear stays.

R.B.

8 July 1899, p. 1105.

I cannot agree with your correspondents who advise that boys also should be laced into stays. I am sure the result would be prejudicial to both their health and manliness. I had the misfortune to be brought up by an aunt who had a strong prejudice against boys. She therefore tried to make me as girlish and effeminate as possible. Every morning and evening I was tightly laced into dainty satin corsets; very great care was taken of my hands and complexion, and my feet were encased in smart pointed high heeled shoes. Indeed, when alone, in the evening, I was sometimes dressed entirely as a girl. In time, I confess, like your other correspondents, I grew to like the sensation of tight lacing but of course, I could never join other boys in athletics of any kind, and my health suffered accordingly. I have at last managed to emancipate myself, and though very reluctantly have given up wearing corsets. I cannot think the beautiful figure, small feet, and soft skin I acquired were any compensation for the many disadvantages entailed by my effeminate education.   MARTYR

22 July 1899, p. 1169.

Like your correspondent 'Martyr' I strongly object to any system of tight-lacing boys, and like him, I can speak with some experience, though happily mine was shorter than his. When I was thirteen I returned home from school to find a stepmother. I was a wild animal. Even my father complained. My stepmother, who was both young and beautiful, undertook to 'tame' me, but refused to say how. One morning when I had been home a week, she took me out for a walk into the town of L....., where we then lived. She wheeled me suddenly into a ladies' outfitting shop. I was unsuspectingly ushered into a sanctum, and in spite of my protests–and I did protest very vigorously–the proprietress and two slim-waisted assistants laced me into a pair of very strongly boned corsets. They were not extremely tight, but they seemed so; while shoulder straps made stooping impossible. A light but strong little chain and lock made it impossible for me to liberate myself. It was very uncomfortable but as my clothes concealed the new figure I had acquired, I did not mind so much. Until I reached the age of seventeen and left school, my holidays were always spent under the corset *régime* and, though I was never systematically tight-laced (the school terms would have interfered), I went about with a far smaller waist than most girls can boast, for I am naturally of a slim build.   TAMED

22 July 1899, p. 1169.

.....It is almost a tradition in my family that both boys and girls should become accustomed to the stay-lace. The boys have always worn, and worn without reluctance, firmly laced stays......   TRAINED IN TIME

22 July 1899, p. 1169.

I will give 'Anxious Mater' my experience as a boy. I was, till ten years of age, a very round-shouldered boy; no shape at all, and was sent to school in Germany to be taught and got into shape. Each morning, after my bath, a thin vest, a pair of thin flannel trousers, and a pair of stays were put on; the latter the governess laced on as tight as she could. Each week they would come in nearly half an inch till my figure got quite respectable, and although at first I rebelled a good deal against it, I soon found that it was most comfortable. I kept the stays on all day and all night, and the only time they came off was when we had our bath. In a short time I had improved wonderfully, had a good figure, and my own people did not know me when I got home. I had two years of this treatment.   MALTA

In 1900 two more correspondents confirmed that stays were worn by boys in their families.

30 June 1900, p. 1073.

My husband has worn corsets at my instigation for over twenty years. My two boys, one now in South Africa as a Yeomanry Volunteer, the other at Oxford, where he excels as a football player, were kept in firmly laced stays while under my care, and now have no intention of giving them up. I am proud of their figures, and hope soon to see their well laced-in waists at my table again.   BEATRICE.

109

Modèles des *Magasins du Louvre*. — TOILETTES D'ÉTÉ POUR ENFANTS. — Modèles des *Magasins du Louvre*.

19.   Summer Costumes for Children.   *La Mode Illustrée*, 10 June 1894, p. 181.

21 July 1900, p. 1168.

For myself, one of a family of nine–four boys and five girls– we were all carefully corseted in our youth, and all of us boys still continue to wear them. I am now twenty-six. G.W.D.

Letters on this subject printed after 1900 have been included in my *Borrowed Plumes*.

VIII
SOCIETY

Society began life in 1879 as *The Mail Budget*, changing its name to *Society* on 12 March 1880. Its first proprietor and editor was George Plant.[1] On 5 July 1890 a new proprietor is named as F.J. Lambert and on 19 July *The Critic* was incorporated. The address was 3, Bolt Court, E.C. Several further changes of publisher and address took place in the nineties. I have noted the following, but there may be others and the dates given may not be the earliest to apply. 6 September 1890: 79-82, Temple Chambers, Bouverie Street; 4 July 1891: General Publishing Company, 280, Strand; 22 August 1901: European Newspaper and Publicity Trust Ltd., 280, Strand; 9 January 1892: 30, Catherine Street, Strand; 4 August 1894: 173, Strand; 16 September 1899: 11/13, Catherine Street, Strand. The theatrical impresario, Sir Charles Cochran (1872-1951), throws some light on the character of the paper and the people running it at the end of the century.

> I met an old gentleman named Eaton Edevain, who ran a more or less disreputable weekly which had a bright yellow cover, and was called *Society*. I gathered that its chief revenue came from the advertisements of massage establishments; that its leading literary feature was a scandalous serial entitled 'The Confessions of Nemesis Hunt'. The author of this serial was my old friend, Reggie Bacchus; it was at his house that I met Edevain. Edevain's son was a well-known baritone, Templer Saxe, who was touring the provinces with the comic opera *Paul Jones*, in which Agnes Huntingdon had made so big a success in London some years earlier. The old man invited me to take over the management of his touring company.[2]

The statements made by Cochran must be treated with caution. I do not think that there were many advertisements for 'massage establishments'. One such was the following on 17 October 1896 (p. 843).

> ELECTRIC BATHS and MASSAGE; Wier-Mitchell's System. Six Lady Masseuses. Patients 11 to 9, and Sundays. Discipline treatment; new system.–20, Great Portland Street, Oxford Street. Manicure and Chiropody. Massage Taught.

What is more important is that on 3 September 1898 the paper began a long series of articles entitled 'Massage in the West End'. Its ostensible purpose was to expose the prostitution which went on under the cover of massage. I cannot say whether the premises at 20, Great Portland Street fell within this category. No doubt Edevain felt that this boosted his sales. When 'The Confessions of Nemesis Hunt' began on 1 April 1899, it was stated to be 'edited by the author of THE HYPOCRITE', a novel published in 1899 which was in fact written by Cyril Ranger Gull, who later wrote many novels under the name, 'Guy Thorne'. Nothing seems to be known about Edevain except that his son was the famous baritone. I am not quite sure whether the 'old man' to whom Cochran refers is Edevain or his son. In either case Edevain must be in middle age or elderly. On the other hand, Mendes does give some information about Bacchus and Gull. Reginald Bacchus was born in June 1873 and was at Exeter College, Oxford from 1893 to 1896. Gull came down from Oxford in 1898 and the two of them shared a flat in Craven Street, off the Strand. According to Mendes, Bacchus, Gull and Hannaford Bennett (another Oxford contemporary) edited *Society* from 1899 to 1900. That would fit in with the change of address noted above.[3]

The contents of *Society* are very similar to those of *Modern Society*: news of, and gossip about, the fashionable world, reviews of books, music and the stage, perhaps less about fashion than in *Modern Society*. Similarly, letters to the editor were published from time to time, notably about corporal punishment and tight-lacing. The first letter about corsets appeared on 16 July 1892 under the heading 'Stays Injurious to Health'. Letters were published on tight-lacing and other subjects in 1894, 1896 and continuously in 1899 and 1900. Many of the letters were well written and surprisingly frank. In August and September 1894 and in 1899 and 1900 there were several letters from men who had been obliged to wear corsets or even complete female attire for one reason or another. Most of these have been included in my *Men In Petticoats*. I now reproduce two more which fall within the scope of the present collection. 'A Lady's Maid' provides further confirmation that in some families boys also wore stays.

1 September 1894, p. 703.

I have read with interest the letters on corsets for men, but as a lady's maid of some experience in the art of figure making I know of many instances of men wearing tightly laced corsets. In one family I was with the mother insisted on boys and girls being laced as tightly as possible, none of the boys being allowed to exceed 19in., or the girls 16in., and the latter had to lace even tighter on occasion. . . .

A LADY'S MAID.

A 'Victim of Stays' was brought up with his twin sister by an aunt who had a horror of boys. He was still dressed as a girl at the age of twelve. At sixteen his figure was trained like his sister's.

CORSETS FOR MEN   8 September 1894, p. 721.

Having read the interesting articles on corsets for men I send my experiences–not so sensational perhaps, but as true as those of my predecessors. A maiden aunt brought up my twin sister and myself on identically the same system. She had a horror of rough schoolboys, so I was taught at home. Even at twelve years of age I had long hair and short frocks, girls' shoes, and my figure encased in close-fitting corsets, laced every morning by the maid when she had dressed my sister. Our shoulders were kept well back in stiff shoulder straps; gloves worn on every visit to the open air completed our irksome clothing. At sixteen my sister came back from her boarding-school with a very slender fashionable figure, the result of sleeping in stays for three months. My own figure was at once enclosed in very stiff, long stays, and in spite of constant indigestion, headaches, and general lassitude, I was gradually compressed till my waist measured under 17 inches (the size of my sister's). Never having mixed with boys, I was quite contented with my life–made up of music and drawing lessons, fencing twice a week, and quiet walks and tennis with my sister. We lived in North Wales, five miles from a town, and only went to London for a short time once a year. At this date I know I was considered a very 'pretty boy', having fair curly hair, large blue eyes, a pale, delicate complexion, upright figure, nipped in, round and slim at the waist, which was always shown off by a tight bodice or jacket, and belt, tiny feet, in high-heeled shoes, and very white girlish hands never allowed to get soiled under pain of severe punishment. At this age, in spite of the pain our stays undoubtedly inflicted on us, we both took an unaccountable pride in our figures, and at eighteen both had waists of sixteen inches. Our aunt died soon after my nineteenth birthday, luckily leaving us comfortably off; my sister married, and my throat being delicate, I spend the winter in Italy, and fill up the summer travelling and cycling. In spite of my twenty-seven years I still lace into nineteen inches, though, of course, concealing the fact by slight padding; so strong is the force of early training that I should feel lost without stays. Hoping this may interest your readers,   VICTIM OF STAYS

P.S. My measurements might interest your readers: 5 ft. 10 in. (in socks); chest, 36 in.; waist, 19 in.; wrist, 7½ in.; muscle, 13½ in.; hips, 35 in; hands, No. 7 glove; feet, small 4's.

The following letter describes such an extreme situation for the little girl that perhaps the information about the boy will be believed.

A TIGHT-LACED CHILD   5 September 1896, p. 718.
Perhaps your readers will scarcely credit, what is indeed a fact, that a tight-laced child is not an unknown thing. Last week I met a very dressy and stylish lady, whose little girl of 7 years was wearing tight-laced corsets. I do not mean the flimsy bodice, or even the whalebone bodice, laced tightly, which some little girls wear, but the little girl I refer to was actually laced in heavily-boned corsets. These corsets were just like a grown woman's stays in miniature, and were simply filled with steel and stiff whalebone. They were very long stays, and clasped the child tightly for their entire length, and were laced in very tightly, encasing the waist, which was extra long, within 12 inches. The little girl just looked like an hour glass. Of course, it was impossible for her to romp about, or loll about in a chair even. Her mother appeared very proud of and kind to her little girl, who appeared healthy and happy. She also had a boy of 13 who was laced in tight stays.   EMMA GORDON.

In 1896 two or three letters described the situation where an unruly boy had been sent away to live with a woman who undertook his reform. This was then effected by constant whipping or birching. One of the correspondents referred to this as being 'under petticoat government'. Three years later in the case of 'B.A.' a new element was introduced: he actually wore petticoats. For the period of his stay he was dressed as a girl.

SHOULD CHILDREN BE BIRCHED?   28 January 1899, p. 1177.
On reading the several interesting letters on this question, an opinion that I have always held to some extent has been strengthened–viz, that a great many ladies have a natural fondness for inflicting corporal punishment; and that, moreover, they are far more particular as to all the little details that go to make it degrading and humiliating than any man would be. I have nothing to say against punishing boys with the rod; most boys deserve it at some time or another, and it does them no harm. Boys ought always, unless quite little, to be punished by one of their own sex; but there is no doubt that to some women whipping a big boy (for preference) is an absolute pleasure; there is a sort of piquancy about it, I suppose.
My own experience of this is probably only one of many that could be met with. When I was just sixteen my father died, leaving me in charge of a stepmother. During the last year of his life, owing to his ill-health, I had been completely spoilt, and was naturally pretty well unmanageable. My stepmother, instead of packing me off to school, took counsel with a lady friend who held rather advanced notions, with the result that I was presently invited to stay at her house. From the moment I arrived I found myself virtually a prisoner, under most rigorous discipline. I was told that I was to be treated exactly as a naughty girl, and consequently I was compelled to dress as a girl. I think Mrs. A. thoroughly enjoyed subjecting me to bodily chastisement, and in addition she made me undergo all sorts of penances and humiliation. I had no chance to run away; I was never allowed out even in the grounds unless accompanied by Mrs. A. or her maid. When the former was absent from the house for any reason, I was locked up in a small room, very often scantily clothed, and sometimes even with my wrists strapped together. When birched, I had to kneel and thank Mrs. A. and kiss the rod; frequently, on the same day that a flogging had been inflicted, and while I was still

sore and smarting, Mrs. A. would lay me over her knees and soundly smack me. Resistance was no good; the maid was simply requisitioned to strap my limbs firmly, and occasionally even to gag me, and extra cuts were given me. After two months I was sent home supposed to be cured, and eventually I went to school, and thence to the University.

I don't know that all this flogging did me any harm; I mention it merely to show what an innate love of flogging some women seem to have by nature. Yours faithfully,
B.A.

From December 1899 to June 1900 the letters come in thick and fast. 'J.B.' confirms that sometimes boys are dressed as girls for punishment, while 'A Believer in Discipline' does not think that enough.

CORPORAL PUNISHMENT   16 December 1899, p. 2110.

The subjects treated of in your correspondence columns have proved most interesting.

The question of corporal punishment has been discussed pretty fully, but not exhaustively, and I would like to point out that there are other methods of punishment used at schools.

I have known cases where boys, as a punishment, have had to wear girl's clothing, even to complete underwear, and also where grown-up girls, of seventeen and upwards, have similarly to appear dressed as a child of four or five, with low-necked, short-sleeved dresses, baby pinafore, and frock reaching to the knees.

Again, cold baths, which, in summer, are a luxury, have been made use of in winter, as a severe punishment for both sexes. Even tight-lacing, as described by some of your correspondents, is used as a punishment.

[He goes on to discuss the measurement of the small waist and make some general comments about punishment, including the fact that some people enjoy being punished.]
J.B.
Brighton.

THE ROD   30 December 1899, p. 2151

I am glad to see by your correspondence columns this week that there are many who still insist on the wholesome discipline of the rod even for the well-grown. In fact I believe from fifteen to twenty to be the age when its application is most needed, for girls as well as boys.

Your correspondent 'J.B.' refers to other kinds of punishment, such as boys having to appear in girls' dress, and big girls of seventeen and upwards in children's frocks of five or six. I doubt if these punishments prove severe to the offenders, although they might be used as a preparation for the birch. It would be interesting to hear the opinion of any of your readers who are experienced in these matters, as to the most effective and convenient preparation and dress, both for boys and girls, on these occasions. I think it is quite evident, from some of your correspondents' letters, that the preparation is an extremely important part of the discipline, and should be carefully carried out in every detail, so that the ordeal may humble as well as pain.

[He goes on to say does not agree with the entire stripping of the culprit; he also thinks corporal punishment should be extended rather than restricted.]
A BELIEVER IN DISCIPLINE

The next correspondent, 'Curb', seems to be the same 'Curb' who wrote several times to *The Family Doctor* (18 April 1891, 7 May 1892 and 30 September 1893). He is now married to someone who is sympathetic to his interests.

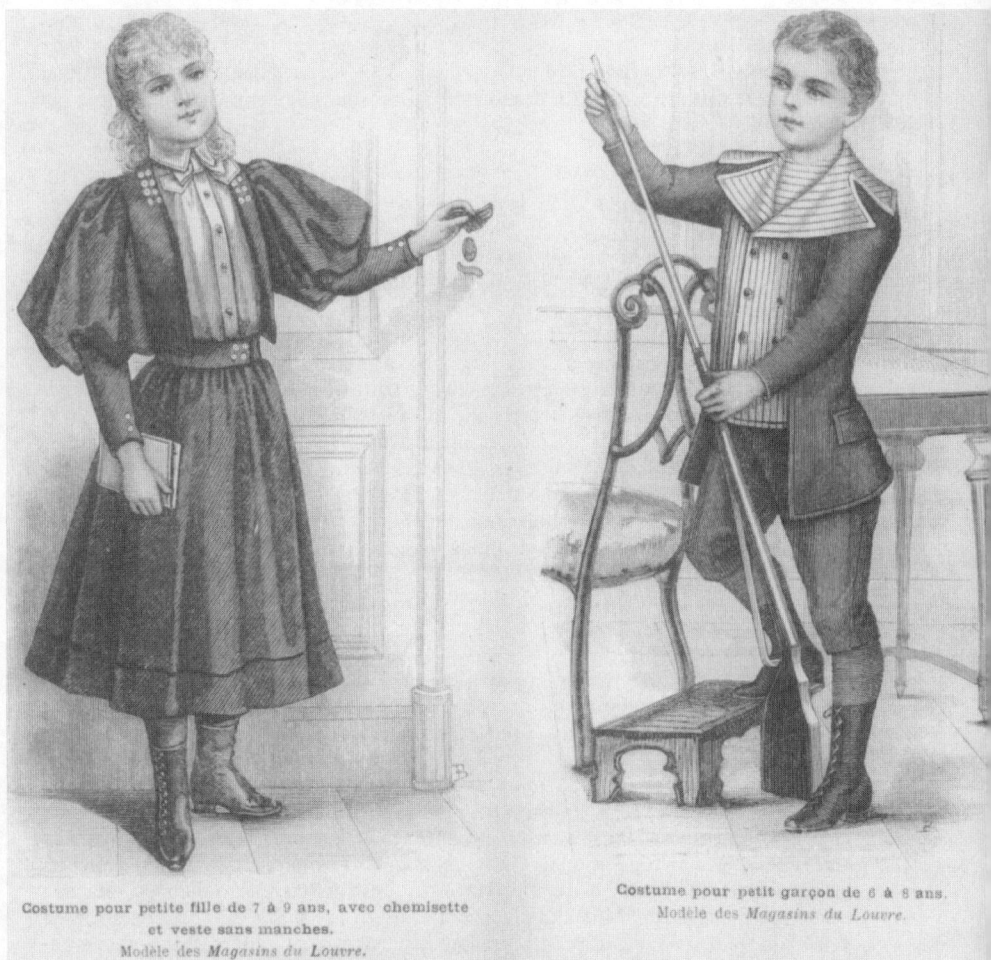

Costume pour petite fille de 7 à 9 ans, avec chemisette
et veste sans manches.
Modèle des *Magasins du Louvre*.

Costume pour petit garçon de 6 à 8 ans.
Modèle des *Magasins du Louvre*.

20.   Costumes for Little Girl of 7 to 9 and Little Boy 6 to 8 Years.
La Mode Illustrée, 21 October 1894, pp. 332-3.

CORSET DISCIPLINE   30 December 1899, p. 2152.
My wife and I have read with great interest the recent letters in your columns on corsets and corporal punishment.

Without going into ridiculous and purely fictitious measurements, I am confident that in figure, hand or foot, you will not find a more perfect votary of fashion than my better half. But she can get through her share of work with any one. We are both thorough believers in smart discipline for either sex, and have both had, in our pupil days, a good experience of it. And now a system of forfeits with redemption by penance keeps us both up to the mark. Naturally, in dress it is she who has most of the submitting to do, whilst in penance she squares the account.

Every girl who is to be a graceful walker should be trained in thin-soled, tight, and pointed boots, with high, narrow heels, good stays, well laced, and an Acme brace or bearing belt, and a governess who does not allow shirking.

For a lad, too, there is nothing more improving than a period of discipline under a lady's rule, and having to render implicit obedience to one less strong than himself, but whose sex prevents retaliation. My own experience is that you do not feel resentment against a pretty martinet, even if the pleasant sense of her power of 'forcing' the improvement of a number of lads, any one of them stronger than herself, should render her at times a trifle tyrannical. I can see myself now in a brown velvet tunic, fitting over a tightly-laced figure, elbows held by the bearing belt, white kid gloves, short knickerbockers, silk stockings, and immensely tight, narrow toed boots, with the most perilous of heels, being drilled on a high day, with a number of others, by a young lady whose slim waist, high-heeled slippers, delicately gloved hands, and easy grace of movement, precluded the idea that our own dress afforded the least excuse for not answering promptly and smartly to any order, whilst a pretty riding switch afforded more sharply tuned persuasion to any delinquent. No one was there to tell us we were ill-used, and it never occurred to us. On the contrary, though we dreaded mademoiselle's displeasure, we were altogether a very happy crew.

Very few people (if a fair driver be only sufficiently smart herself) will admire her the less because her horses chafe at the irksome restraint of tensely-drawn bearing-reins, or because to make them arch their glossy necks the more she holds them tightly in with a severe bit; or, who, in a circus, gets more applause than the *haute école* lady, in the tight-fitting habit, whose skirt conceals the stinging spur that she knows how to use so well? Yours truly,   CURB

'M.F.C.' was unruly and troublesome. His aunt decided to take 'sterner measures', and from the age of thirteen to sixteen he wore girls' underclothing, stays and shoes.

CORSET DISCIPLINE   3 February 1900, pp. 39-40.
Perhaps my experience of corset discipline may be of value to the readers of your interesting paper. When I was thirteen years old, I was left in the care of a maiden aunt. Though I was a slim, good-looking boy, of rather effeminate appearance, I had been at a rough boarding school, and had become ill-mannered, noisy and wild. I was never tidy, and always getting into some scrape or other. My aunt was at first very lenient to me, but I became so troublesome that she resolved to take sterner measures. She consulted with a friend, and went out for a long afternoon's shopping. The next morning she came into my room, and told me I was to wear girls' underclothing beneath my knickerbockers and jacket. Accordingly, in spite of my protests, I was forthwith initiated into the mysteries of dainty lace lingerie, which, I confess, felt very soft and comfortable [presumably a chemise and a pair of drawers]. I was then very tightly laced into a pair of well-cut, firmly-boned satin stays. These produced a strange feeling of restraint, compression and support, which I afterwards grew to like. When

I looked at myself in the glass, I could hardly recognise my straight, shapely figure, and pretty, rounded girlish waist. I also had to wear openwork silk hosiery, and force my feet into smart patent leather shoes, with high heels and pointed toes.

Of course, dressed like this, I could no longer romp or run wild, and at first I constantly rebelled. I soon thought better of it, however, as my aunt instantly punished any outbreak by making me wear pair of shoes I could only just squeeze on, with the most extravagantly-high heels, and by lacing me relentlessly into a pair of 16-inch corsets, which caused me considerable pain. I soon learnt to behave myself, and in a few weeks began quite to like the sensation of wearing stays, and to look forward to putting on the new and smaller pair with which my aunt provided me every two months. I found it advisable to keep my stays on at night, and then I did not have to do so much pulling-in in the morning, and at the end of a year, a fashionable French girl, with an up-to-date maid, would have envied my perfect figure and waist, which was never allowed to exceed seventeen inches, night or day. I was disciplined in this way until I was nearly sixteen, with the most beneficial result to my character and manners, and my health was excellent the whole time. I am sure anyone who is burdened with an unruly, ill-mannered boy, cannot do better than imitate my aunt's system of discipline. Yours truly,   M.F.C.   Gordon Square, W.C.

Immediately after this letter the editor inserted this comment: 'This is one of many other letters which I have received of a similar nature. The writer seems to be as unmanly and effeminate as his aunt is idiotic. What a pity it is there is no conscription, if only to get M.F.C. sent to the front to do a little healthy fighting.' It is particularly interesting that the letter is one of many. The editor's disapproval sounds genuine and in effect adds validity to the letter itself. There follows a letter which challenges belief. It purports to be from a woman who is now subjecting her stepson to the discipline of girls' underwear, stays, boots and gloves.

TIGHT LACING   28 April 1900, pp. 282-3.
I have been extremely interested in your correspondence columns, and really consider the same the most interesting part of your paper. The letter from 'M.F.C.' in a recent issue, describes treatment very similar to what I have had to administer to my step-son. I am only a few years his senior, consequently he much disliked the idea of his father marrying again, and became most insulting and unruly. Consequently, though a big boy, aged 16 years, I resolved upon "taming" him. I therefore consulted my French maid, and decided to put him into a knicker suit, also to insist on his wearing girls' underclothing, bedecked with plenty of lace frills, corsets (tightly fitting) and very high leg button boots, with 3 in. French heels. Both in the measuring and fitting of the above lines, the services of the female household had to be requisitioned, but, having made up my mind to thoroughly subdue him, and have him dressed like a little boy, I was determined it should be carried out. After the 22 in. corset was laced on him, and his feet and calves firmly encased in tight boots, buttoning almost up to his knees, and with extra high heels, he could not offer much resistance. His tunic fits tightly over his corset, and the sleeves reach only just below the elbow, under which pass the upper part of tight-fitting kid gloves. His knickers also fit closely down to the knee, consequently his figure is shown off to advantage. My maid curls his hair daily, also attends to the lacing of his corset, and the buttoning up of his boots, and smartens him up generally. Already he is very much subdued, and really presents a very smart appearance. I intend reducing his waist measurement 1 in. per month, and tomorrow he will be fitted for high boots, with 4 in. French heels. I shall make good use of him as an attendant page to lace my corset, which measures only 17 in. and also button up my boots and gloves; the former, I might state, also have 4 in. heels, and button high in the leg, almost to the knee, and the gloves are also 18-button length, consequently, assistance is necessary, and it relieves my maid. He is now being taught how to make

up my hair. On my lady friends coming to see me, I have him brought in by the maid, and made to stand on a chair for the general admiration of those present. This he greatly resents, and it caused him to blush deeply. I am sure any step-mother who is blessed with an unruly step-son could not do better than to follow my treatment, which she would find would soon bring him to his senses. I should be most happy to give any further particulars to those of your readers who desire. Apologising for the length of this letter, and sincerely hoping you will insert it, as I am sure it would interest many. I remain, yours very truly,   AMY CANNING
Kensington, W., April 12, 1900

In May the editor favoured his readers with this announcement, which indicates the intense interest felt by readers in this subject, and, in particular, in the letter from Amy Canning.

NOTICE TO CORRESPONDENTS   12 May 1900, p. 322.
TO CORRESPONDENTS GENERALLY ON TIGHT-LACING.–A very large number of letters have been received on this subject, many of which are held over for want of space, while others cannot be used from lack of evidence of good faith, caused by absence of real name and address, though several exhibit considerable brilliancy and are worthy of attention. It should be distinctly understood that the appearance of any letters under this head is no evidence that they are endorsed by the Editor.

The Editor further begs to repeat the notice previously given, viz., that he absolutely refuses to become the channel of communication between correspondents or readers. Several epistles have lately been received, with a view to their being forwarded to Mrs. Canning, whose letter appeared, three weeks since, in these columns. They accordingly remain undelivered.

The Editor did, however, print the following letter immediately after the foregoing announcement.

I have read in your last issue the interesting letter of Mrs. Amy Canning, and would be glad if she would write more fully regarding the training of her stepson. To begin with, she does not state by what means the resistance of her stepson was overcome. Did the female household commence by tying his hands behind him, in order to lace on his corset? Are any means adopted to prevent him slackening his stay-lace, or undoing his gloves, when left to himself? Has Mrs. Canning provided him with a governess at home, or how is his education conducted? What are his various forms of punishment, and by whom and how administered? A detailed description of these would be very useful to us readers. Personally, I think the idea excellent, and very beneficial to lots of lounging, uncouth lads, and would be only too glad to hear of a detailed system for rigidly carrying it out. Does Mrs. Canning make her stepson sleep in his corset, and, if so, what means are taken to prevent his tampering with his stay-lace during the night? Hoping you will insert this letter, in order that Mrs. Canning may give us definite details, and thanking you in anticipation. Yours truly,
EMILY BROWNING
Stirling, April 28, 1900.

Of the many letters mentioned by the editor, he printed several, some denouncing Amy Canning, others expressing approval and interest.

12 May 1900, p. 323.
I have read with horror the letter signed 'Amy Canning' in your issue of this week.

119

It seems to me well-nigh incredible that a young matron can be deliberately guilty of such degrading treatment, even to an unruly stepson.

What does your correspondent imagine can be the fate of a young man brought up in the way she describes? I prefer to think that such an attractive young lady has been thoughtless, rather than intentionally cruel, and that, now that her stepson has been subdued, she will be as merciful as she has been strong, and relieve the unfortunate youth from further degradation.

[He also criticised strongly the cruel treatment meted out to some girl victims of tight-lacing described in the correspondence.]   CYRIL A. BLUNT
1, Cullum Street, London, E.C. [occupiers, Sprott and Lehmann, hairdressers.],
April 25, 1900.

NOTICES TO CORRESPONDENTS   19 May 1900, p. 342.

AMY CANNING. I cannot under any circumstances, accede to your request to put correspondents in communication with each other. It is open to you to append your address to your letters for publication.

GERALD CANNING. I have always made it a rule to give no addresses whatever. The annual subscription is 6s. 6d., payable in advance.

CORPORAL PUNISHMENT   19 May 1900, p. 342.

Kindly forward, after filling in the proper address, my letter to Mrs. Amy Canning.* I have been a constant reader of *Society* for some years, and have been much interested in your correspondence columns on corporal punishment. For some time I have been troubled with my boy, who is aged fifteen. He is very troublesome, but, thanks to your correspondent's advice, which I acted upon, I am glad to say he is a better boy today. Amy Canning gives this week, I note, excellent advice for subduing an unruly boy. If any of your readers would like to reply to this letter, which I hope you will find room for in your columns, I should be happy to answer any questions. I should especially like to hear from 'G.H.', of Birkenhead [birched by women, 10 February 1900], and 'H.J.', of Okehampton, who wrote 'Cousin Frank's Reply,' also 'Eleanor S.,' who wrote some verses in your issue of Sept. 9. I enclose some lines, original, which I trust you will deem fit for publication. (Lack of space prevents their appearance. ED.) I am, dear Sir, yours faithfully,   MRS. H. HAMILTON.
Richmond, April 26, 1900.

*(The Editor begs to repeat that his rule is never to place correspondents in communication with each other.)

19 May 1900, p. 342.

I am very much interested in your correspondent's (Amy Canning) account of her treatment of her unruly stepson.

As this, in some measure, coincides with the discipline which I experienced at the hands of a stepmother, I shall be very glad to have fuller details, and would reciprocate by relating my own. I am, dear Sir, yours faithfully,   J. WILBY.
Brighton.

In the next issue, 'G.J.M.' gives another example of punishment actually going on at the present time. Chastisement having no effect on his son, his sister-in-law offers to take him in hand. She brings him under control by successively imposing girls' stays and shoes, boots, a blouse and finally threatening petticoats instead of knickerbockers.

CORPORAL PUNISHMENT   26 May 1900, p. 361.

While spending an evening at my club last week, I came across a recent issue of

ONLY AT 62 BOLD STREET LIVERPOOL

Vandyke

LIVERPOOL

vii.   Family Photograph. Liverpool, mid-eighties. (The girl is in mourning.)

viii.   Family Photograph. Valparaiso. Inscribed on back:
'To Mr and Mrs Peak with a Mason's Love.' 10/9/84.

Society, giving an account of a punishment to a lad, by means of corsets and other articles of feminine attire, and, having been witness recently of a great success by almost identical means–in fact the likeness is remarkable–I think it might be of interest to your readers to have an account of same. My son came home from boarding-school last Christmas with an intimation from his headmaster that he was not to return. Gross impertinence and disobedience, together with exhibitions of violent temper, were not stopped at all by severe birchings and canings at the hands of his master at college, and, in short, they had had enough of him. I found before a week had elapsed that bad as he had been during the summer vacation he was worse now, and his delight lay in torturing his younger brothers and swearing at the servants. Finding thrashing of no use, and kindness worse, I was looking about for a suitable school of extreme strictness, when my sister-in-law, who resides in the neighbouring town, offered to try her hand. As she seemed pretty confident, I gave her *carte blanche* for a fortnight, during which I had to be in London–I may explain that I am a widower–and on my return I found a total change in the lad, who is getting on for 15 years. It appears that on the first morning the boy was seized, immediately after his bath, by his aunt and three servants, and, in spite of his struggling, was laced into a pair of very stiffly-boned stays, measuring 20 inches round the waist, but left open the first day about two inches. His shoulders were braced back tightly by some attachment to the corsets, and a pair of pointed leather shoes with high heels were fastened on. He was allowed free liberty to go where he liked, but couldn't remove his stays, owing to a metal band, nor his shoes, as he was so braced up he couldn't reach the laces. He, however, spoiled these latter by burning the heels through the bars of the grate. So next morning, before he woke, he was again seized, and, in spite of his struggling, his waist was compressed another inch, and a pair of high-leg, button boots, with very high heels, was substituted for the shoes. Some difficulty in walking was occasioned thereby, as, besides the awkwardness of negotiating the heels, the boots were very tight; but the boy's revenge came in breaking several articles, as a punishment for which his corsets were laced close, and instead of his jacket he had to wear a white blouse, belonging to one of my sister-in-law's daughters, altered somewhat to fit, and belted in round the waist, at the same time being warned that any further misconduct would be met by the substitution of petticoats for his knickers. This was the last straw, he didn't so much mind the stays, as they scarcely showed, except when he had the blouse on without a coat over, but he was ashamed of his 'girl's boots', and he wouldn't risk anything else. Though free to go where he liked, he kept indoors lest he should meet any of his boy friends, and when I returned late one night, I went to his bedroom and found him quite cured and gentlemanly. It was agreed that he should come to dinner next evening in his punishment attire, pending his release as reformed, and, when he entered the dining room, he looked greatly changed for the better, instead of untidy clothes, dirty collar and tie, and muddy boots, he was wearing a tight-fitting, white silk blouse, with a very slender girlish waist, closely confined by a neat, black belt, white kid gloves, long buttoned up the arm, black knickers, altered, of course, to fit his newly-shaped waist, black silk stockings, and small, very high-heeled boots of *glacé* kid, buttoned high up the leg. He had changed in manners too, and remained after dinner to a pleasant chat, showing himself an altered lad in every respect. I decided that once every week he was to come to dinner garbed as he was then, but could otherwise go back to boy's dress, and he politely thanked me and retired. Since then he has only once needed correction, and on being given a choice of a week's similar punishment or a flogging, he chose the former, and, to me, much pleasanter alternative. This month–May–he is to discard the attire entirely, even the weekly dinner dress, so that the clothes, etc., will be kept entirely for corrective purposes.

I can recommend this treatment, therefore, for unruly boys, but I think your correspondent was quite unnecessarily cruel in exhibiting her step-son so clothed to her lady-friends.

Hoping this is not too long, and enclosing my name, not for publication. Yours truly, G.J.M.
Hotel Victoria, April 30, 1900.

Letters were still coming in and the editor printed another announcement. He also printed another letter from Amy Canning.

NOTICE TO CORRESPONDENTS 2 June 1900, p. 381.
A large number of letters, relating to tight-lacing, punishment by means of change of garb, punishment of children, etc., are held over for want of space.
J.R.F. Room will be given for your letter in next week's issue.

TIGHT LACING, ETC., AS A PUNISHMENT 2 June 1900, p. 381.
I notice in today's issue of your valuable paper that you publish the addresses of correspondents if desired, I therefore give you my address, as below, which you will greatly oblige by publishing with this letter, so that those correspondents who desire to communicate with me, in reference to my letter, which you were good enough to publish in a recent issue of your paper, may have an opportunity of doing so.

I am glad that my remarks on how to treat unruly boys have been of so much interest to your readers, and that several intend applying the same treatment to their own sons, which I am sure they will find most beneficial. How one of your correspondents can describe as 'degrading' the smart dress treatment I have applied to my stepson, I cannot understand. I am sure that, if I was to submit him to the gaze of your readers, that they would admit that his appearance is decidedly smart. He was an extremely ill-mannered and untidy youth before I took him in hand, and I am sure that he has vastly improved in every way. I have no intention at present of altering his mode of outfit, as I am convinced that a year or two of discipline treatment, by means of ladies' pattern corsets, high-leg boots, with extra-high French heels, long, tight-fitting kid gloves, etc., will improve his figure immensely, and also compel him to pay that respect to the sex which is generally termed the weaker one. For the benefit of your other correspondent, I might mention that his sleeping corsets measure two inches more than his day ones–that is, 24 inches. His day corsets will be reduced gradually to 18 inches; this, I think, quite small enough, as I am not anxious to injure his health. He is now exercised daily by the maid, in his high-leg boots, with 4-inch French heels, and is beginning to acquire quite a graceful carriage. His punishments are many and varied, ranging from a sound birching, to the insertion of lace frills in the bottom of his knickers, and lace collars and cuffs. Occasionally, for a minor offence, I have a face mask put on him, thus serving the double purpose of punishing him, and improving his complexion. I should be glad if your correspondents, Mrs. Hamilton and J. Wilby, will write me, together with any other of your readers who have put their sons or stepsons through this smart discipline treatment.

Apologising for the length of this letter, and trusting you will insert same in answer to the many correspondents to whom my previous letter appears to have been of such interest. I remain, dear Sir, yours truly, AMY CANNING
*22, Eldon Street, London, E.C., May 15, 1900.
(*It is to be distinctly understood that the Editor holds himself in no way responsible for the bona-fides of any correspondent.)

The editor was right to be suspicious about the address given. In her first letter Amy Canning had written from Kensington. According to the *Post Office Directory for 1898*,

122

the occupier of 22, Eldon street was Louis Valendin Hose, hairdresser. On the other hand the next correspondent pointed out that Amy Canning's methods were described in a German book of 1848. He also claimed that this treatment is still applied in Germany. In the same issue, 'High Heels' asked Amy Canning for more information.

'BRING UP A CHILD IN THE WAY HE SHOULD GO.'   2 June 1900, p. 381.
   Your correspondent's account of the correction of her unruly stepson is by no means a new method, for a similar account is to be met with in a small treatise on The Discipline in the Family, translated from the German of Moellen, and published in 1848. A number of different methods for correcting children are given in this little work, but the authoress herself strongly recommends the use of the birch, both as a corrective, and also for promoting the health of children of both sexes.
   I may add that Mrs. Amy Canning's treatment is still resorted to in Germany, or, certainly was some ten years since.   FREDK. T. HIBGAME.
Beaufort House, Clifton Wood, Bristol,
May 16, 1900.

   This looks like, and is, a genuine name and address and can be found in the contemporary Bristol Directories. Unfortunately I have been unable to trace the German book mentioned or its translation.

HIGH HEELS AND TIGHT LACING   2 June 1900, p. 382.
   After being from home for some time, on my return I read with great interest the numerous letters in *Society* on tight-lacing. I think the course adopted by Mrs. Canning a most excellent one, and I hope she will give us some more particulars. What does her stepson wear out-of-doors? If Mrs. Canning was to have a photograph, excluding the face, taken of the boy, many of your readers would be glad to purchase one, which could be done through a good firm of photographers.
   [She continues about her own corsets and high-heeled boots and shoes. Her husband wears indoors a ladies' size 4 boot or shoe with 4-in. heels]   HIGH HEELS

   The following is the letter for which space was promised the previous week. The editor's heading suggests that he is sceptical but amused. The main difficulty is the time scale. Would there have been time to do what is stated in the time available since Amy Canning's letter on 28 April 1900?

AMAZING!   9 June 1900, p. 401.
   Like many readers of your interesting paper, I have been struck by the letters in your correspondence column. There can be no doubt that boys between sixteen and seventeen are at a very awkward age. They are apt to think themselves already men, and resent all control, especially feminine. It is a period of conceit, which becomes more than ever pronounced in cases where lads have not been sent to public schools, to meet with superiors and rivals.
   In such cases a compulsory return to knickerbockers and a punishment dress are of undoubted benefit, as I can show by an instance which was founded upon Mrs. Amy Canning's example. I showed her letter to a lady friend, living a few miles from London, who had been given absolute control of a boy of that age, while his relatives were away in India. It was their wish that he should be educated privately by tutors, and not sent to a school where he would soon have found his level. My friend was at her wits' end to know what to do to check his impertinence and misbehaviour. She did not at first put much confidence in Mrs. Canning's plan, but she thought over it, and, when I went down to see her yesterday, I found that she had put it into practice, with a few

21.   Costumes for Children.   *La Mode Illustrée*, 3 May 1896, p.139.

changes, however, which I thought might prove of interest to your readers, particularly since the results have exceeded her expectations.

She had a white serge knickerbocker suit made to his measurement, but without his knowledge. It was made to fit tightly over corsets, and the sleeves reached only just below the elbow, as Mrs. Canning described. She had also a pair of patent leather shoes made from his boot trees, only tighter, and with very high heels, and bought his corsets, stockings and gloves. As soon as her purchases had come home, she told him just before tea-time what she had done, and that his new dress was laid out for him upon his bed, and that he must go and put it on before he had his tea.

This he refused to do in a most insulting way until she threatened to call in the servants to help her. She had even rung the bell with that object, but, seeing no escape, he then gave in, more surprised at my friend's firmness than realising his subjection. However, in half-an-hour he came back to the drawing-room very much ashamed and subdued. He had hooked together his corsets which had previously been laced to the intended measurement, he wore the white serge suit, long white kid gloves, buttoned up his wrists and arms, white silk stockings on his legs, and the high-heeled patent leather shoes which had been ornamented with bows and silver buckles. My friend then complimented him upon his appearance, which was greatly improved, and told him that he need not wear the clothes in the morning or afternoon, as she did not wish to interfere with his lessons or recreations, but that he must be ready dressed in this way every evening by 5.30, and submit to her control till bed-time. He was warned, besides, that any disobedience would be punished, as she could no longer put up with his misconduct, and that if he persevered in it, a governess would be substituted for his tutors, and he would have to wear the punishment dress all day. His clothes, stockings, etc., were chosen white because one of his tricks was to slip out of the house in the evening and pull down the signboards of any houses to let, and otherwise annoy the neighbours; now, however, his dress would show any soil or stain, and, if he wished to escape punishment, he had to keep quiet and behave in an orderly way.

The lad seemed to feel his position very keenly, and, for a day or two, gave no reason for complaint. But one evening he did not come home until eight, refused to give any explanation, and again was only induced to put on his knickerbocker suit by the threat of force. His knickers, I should mention, reach down to the knee, but do not cover it, being buttoned closely just above, and over the silk stockings, which thus clothe him from above the knees to the insteps. My friend determined to punish his rebellion at once, and, after tea, took him to her own boudoir. There she asked him whether he would patiently take his punishment from her, or whether he preferred the extra ignominy of having the servants as witnesses. Seeing that she was in earnest, he sullenly agreed to submit to her. My friend thereupon laced his corsets an inch tighter, and made him put on a pair of buckled shoes, which she had ready for the emergency, similar to those he was wearing, only much tighter, and with much higher heels. She then strapped his kid-gloved hands firmly together, and ordered him sharply to sit down in a chair, and hold out his ankles. This he did very reluctantly, begging to be let off, and promising better behaviour. But my friend was obdurate, believing that nothing short of his complete submission would be of any use, and she did not move until he was at last seated, stretching out his feet obediently to her. She then tied his ankles with a handkerchief, but not so tightly as to hurt him, but with a piece of thin cord she fastened the high heels of his shoes as tightly as she could draw them together. He was then made to stand straight up, in a position where she could see him from head to foot, and forbidden to move a muscle. In a very little time the discomfort and shame of his attitude brought him to his senses, and he begged most humbly for pardon. But he was kept standing for half-an-hour, after which period he was allowed to sit down, but his hands and feet were not untied until his bed-time, and, in addition, his eyes

were blindfolded. One or two other punishments she found necessary, but, in the main, since that time, his conduct has steadily improved, and my friend believes that she will soon be able safely to slacken her hold on him. But since neither his lessons nor his riding and athletics are interfered with, she is in no hurry, appreciating his unfamiliar docility of manners and liking too the smartness of his appearance. Apologising for the length of this letter, which I think will interest those of your correspondents who have made enquiries upon the subject, I remain, yours faithfully,   J.R.F.
London, W., May 22, 1900.

In the same issue is a letter about training people to wear high heels. The reference to boys is surprising, but the writer seems to know what she is talking about.

HIGH HEELS AND POINTED TOES   9 June 1900, pp. 401-2.
Having had very considerable experience both in wearing high heels and pointed toes, and in superintending the wearing of them for training purposes, I will endeavour to explain to 'Ladybird' their especial advantage, for the especial advantage comes in the great assistance given in producing a pretty and dainty walk.

No one who saw *The Belle of New York*, at the Shaftesbury, could fail to notice the exquisite step of Miss Edna May when wearing the white dress in the second act, but only the initiated would appreciate how much she was assisted in it by the very high heels and extremely pointed toes of the beautiful tight shoes, of which the short skirt allowed a clear view, and enabled one to note, at the same time, how well she kept her knees back and taut. It is in this keeping back of the knees that the novice in very high-heel wearing finds his or her greatest trouble, whilst rigorous enforcement is a most important duty of the teacher.

I do not preach what I do not practise, and would never dream of entering a ballroom without shoes just as high-heeled, tight, and pointed as those of Miss May.

Of course, to a lad who has been accustomed to slummock as he likes in big, broad, thick boots, to be suddenly shod in this way, and expected to walk according to the example of a lady teacher, is somewhat of an ordeal. Still it is surprising how quick a change can be developed when the teacher is insistent, and, whilst encouraging all progress, quickens up any carelessness with a light riding switch, against which a silk stocking affords only moderate defence. But to produce the best effect, the pupil must be otherwise well in hand, a high collar to prevent following the toes with the nose, well corseted, tight shoulder braces, and the bearing-belt to keep the elbows well at home. The high heels and pointed toes will at first lead the pupil to take over short steps, but the switch will soon cure that, if needed, and then between the two the dainty step required will be learned with wonderful readiness. It is just similar in principle to teaching a lady's saddle horse a pretty prancing style, by holding him tightly in with a powerful Hanoverian bit, so as to arch his neck, and set him well over his hind legs, whilst he is compelled to keep well up to it by the generous use of a good stinging spur. Yours truly,   YLDIE

The last three correspondents all express their reactions to Amy Canning. The middle one is hostile, but the other two approve and talk about what they would like to do on the same lines.

FIGURE TRAINING, DISCIPLINE, ETC.   16 June 1900, p. 422.
I have read with great interest the correspondence which has been appearing in your interesting paper. I think it is a pity, considering the number of letters you apparently receive, that you do not devote more space to correspondence. I have read with much pleasure the letters of Mrs. Amy Canning, but I, like Emily Browning, am disap-

pointed she does not enter into more detail. I think her idea is most excellent, but, as I said before, lacks detail.

Nothing, to my mind, is so adaptable to untidy, boisterous boys as to humiliate them by subjecting them to a rigid system of petticoat government.

I am now living with my sister, who has lately become a widow, and in delicate health. She has three boys and two girls, ranging from 16½ to 11, a girl being the youngest. As the duty of looking after them will now practically devolve on me, I wish to employ the best method, and exercise the strictest and most rigid discipline. The boys, at present, are at school. My idea is to remove them, and employ the strictest of governesses. I know a man in the army who passed into Woolwich directly from a governess. He is a most remarkably nice gentleman, and though he will not tell me all his experiences, has informed me that while under his governess hardly a week passed without his being strapped down and severely flogged by his governess, who mostly always used a lady's riding whip, the usual number of cuts being thirty, and sometimes considerably more. She used also to make him wear a silk handkerchief tied in a faultless bow round his neck, which he did not like at all, while his hands were frequently securely tied behind his back for considerable periods. Whether his system is right or wrong, I can only say it has been a success in his case.

I think the plan of putting boys in corsets night and day excellent, and would like to hear the experience in a detailed manner of any lady or boy who has employed or been subjected to the *régime*.

How, and by what means, is tampering with the stay-lace detected and dealt with? Gloves, boots, and frilled knickers protruding below short, cut-away trousers are good, and even girls' dress entire, backboards and stocks. All these methods I wish to employ with my nephews if anybody will kindly send me information.

I admit your correspondence has rather given me a penchant for humiliating my nephews, and with my staff of maids, will be interesting to carry out, and in course of time, will gladly, in return for your assistance, send an account of their training. Yours truly,   EVELYN SCOTT (LADY)
Brechin, 31 May, 1900.

Near the beginning of a long letter about her own and her sisters' figure training a girl refers to Amy Canning as follows.

16 June 1900, p. 422.

I think Amy Canning's conduct abominable, not to say indecent. I am one of a family of four girls and four boys, and I certainly think that all boys should go to boarding school, as my brothers did. They enjoy the games, comradeship, etc., and the discipline is the best thing in the world for them. As to the future of boys treated like Mrs. Canning's, it is too sad to think of, and every man I have shown her letter to has agreed with me.   ONE OF FOUR

TIGHT-LACING AND OTHER PUNISHMENTS   23 June 1900, p. 442.

I was much interested in the letter from Amy Canning* in the correspondence columns of this week's issue, especially as a great friend of mine (a widow lady) is blest with a son to whom treatment of the kind described by your correspondent would be very applicable. Her son is incorrigible, and on several occasions, at her request, I have had to administer a good birching to him, but without any very satisfactory results.

I have discussed the matter with her, and she has decided that as he is quite beyond her control she would much like to place him in a boarding school conducted by a lady who is a strict disciplinarian, and where the boys are put through a course of figure training, similar to what has been described by some of your correspondents, namely, the wearing of knicker suits, stiff corsets (ladies' pattern), tight-fitting, high-leg boots with extra high French heels, long, tight-fitting kid gloves, etc.

Her son is now just turned sixteen years of age, and thinks himself quite the man, aping the ways and manners of his elders, and has supreme contempt for the other sex, therefore it would humiliate him greatly to have to submit to wearing a costume in which the above-mentioned articles would be the most conspicuous part of his attire. We are both convinced that a year or two of this treatment would thoroughly reform him, and, at the same time smarten up his appearance generally.

My friend would be very glad if some of your correspondents could inform her where she could place her son to undergo this special treatment, also, if they would fully describe the costume worn in such schools, and the rules for the general discipline of the establishments. Also when special punishment is necessary whether the birch is resorted to, or whether the culprit is dressed in extra humiliating costume; the latter she thinks would be most beneficial in the case of her son.

I must apologise for the length of this letter, but sincerely trust that you will insert same, and thereby be of the greatest assistance to my friend, and for which she will be very grateful. I am, Sir, yours faithfully,   J.K.N.

Maida Vale, W.

(*This letter was received anterior to the date of Mrs. Canning's last letter. ED.)

There were no further letters after 30 June 1900. On 7 July 1900 a new owner is announced, The Society Press Ltd., 167, Temple Chambers, and the character of the paper changes, but the paper does not long survive the change. The last issue is for 3 November 1900. An attempt was made to restart the paper as a monthly from 30 March 1901 at 77, Chancery Lane, but it ran for only six issues.

1   *The New Cambridge Bibliography of English Literature*, edited by George Watson, 5 vols (Cambridge: C.U.P., 1969-1977) III, 1815.
2   Charles Cochran, *The Secrets of a Showman* (London: William Heinemann, [1925]), p. 79, cited by Peter Mendes, *Clandestine Erotic Fiction in English 1800-1930* (Aldershot: Scolar Press, 1993), p. 342.
3   Mendes, pp. 27, 340-2. The serial was elaborated by Bacchus into a classic of erotic literature, *The Confessions of Nemesis Hunt* (1902).

IX

CONCLUSION

In spite of the dozens of letters about corset discipline for boys and the punitive effect of girl's dress entire, there is very little confirmation or acknowledgement of this in biographies or works on social history and costume. If the incidents reported are true, I suspect that both parties to the punishment were reticent about what went on. I have already mentioned Curzon's red calico petticoat, but this was not revealed to the public until Leonard Mosley's biography of 1960. I have reproduced further letters on this subject up to 1912 in my *Borrowed Plumes*, and there is much more to come right up to 1941. Much of this later correspondence will in fact relate to events before 1900, but there is no way of dating the alleged events with any certainty. Nevertheless the impression I get is that this punishment held sway, even if only as a threat, for about fifty years up to the First World War, almost but not quite dying out by the time of the Second World War. In this concluding chapter I wish to cite what other evidence or references I have been able to find covering the nineteenth century. Such references can be found in the writings of psychologists, in memoirs and in fiction.

Havelock Ellis provides an example of the threat in his case history of 'T.S.', a successful author, fifty years of age. 'In appearance he is tall, with the air of an English gentleman of sensitive refinement. There is nothing obviously feminine about him.'

The wish to wear the clothes of the other sex is my earliest definite recollection. My father's calling compelled frequent moves from place to place, and he kept a diary; I am therefore able to give essential dates with a measure of precision. I was between six and eight years old when I used to lie in bed imagining myself dressed in skirts; I invariably saw myself as a grown woman in black. This seems to me singular, as I love bright colours.

I think this train of thought, which has never left me, arose through my mother's treatment. She cordially disliked me and was at pains to prove her antipathy; she beat me frequently and mercilessly; and if she could humiliate me before my brothers and sisters, did it. A favourite taunt was a threat to dress me in my sister's clothes; the threat was never carried out–I suspect my father interfered–but when a child is perpetually ill-used and such a threat occurs daily, he falls into a habit of brooding over injustices, and my broodings in the bed to which I was so often sent 'to be out of my sight', took the form stated. I was made to part my hair in the middle 'like a baby girl', and my resemblance to a girl was consistently pressed upon me. With what justice I do not know; there is no photograph of me at this age.

My mother, however, was a very shrewd judge of character, and it may be that I was feminine looking ('He ought to be a girl,' she would say), and this offended her instincts; hers as a strong character. . . . I was between fifteen and sixteen, home for holidays, when I first donned girl's clothes. My elder sister dressed me, and I remember her regret that my hair was not long enough to be curled as then 'nobody could guess you're not a girl'. It was about this time that the master of the school I was at sneered at me, saying I ought to dress as a girl and be at a girls' school. This could only have been a gibe at my appearance, for I was as keen about football and other games–also mischief–as the rest. Nobody knew of my craving to wear girls' dress; nothing on earth would have persuaded me to reveal it.[1]

We do not know when Ellis interviewed 'T.S.' and obtained this narrative but it was cer-

129

Costume pour petit garçon de 4 à 5 ans.　Robe pour petite fille de 5 à 6 ans.
(Les fig. 21 à 30, *recto*, appart.
à ce costume.)
Modèles des *Magasins
du Louvre*.

22.　Costumes for Little Boy of 4 to 5 and Little Girl 5 to 6 Years.

La Mode Illustrée, 14 May 1899, p. 238.

tainly after the First World War and before 1928. He was probably born around 1875 and the threats of girls' clothes would have been made in the eighteen-eighties. An episode in the childhood of 'Howard N.' born in those years shows how the idea of this punishment can be suggested to parents. His family went to live in France before he was seven and he was probably eight or nine when they returned to the U.S.A.

One day on the way back to the United States I was cold and my mother wanted to put on a red, crocheted wool petticoat and I didn't. I scorned it. They would put the petticoat over my coat when I would do anything naughty and I would be ashamed. Even later in life when I felt ashamed I had the feeling I had lost caste with somebody in my family. I would get a glimpse of myself walking away with this petticoat flapping against my legs.[2]

The following example is slightly outside our period but it is a good illustration of the sort of thing which was done and accepted at the turn of the century. The subject was a man of thirty-six, born in the U.S.A. about 1900.

At the age of six, when he first began to go to school, he wore girl's clothes at a school show. Four or five months later he soiled his pants and his mother made him wash the pants and wear girl's clothes for months. He remembers being so shy and humiliated that when visitors came he would hide under the table.[3]

Writing in 1913, the American anthropologist Elsie Clews Parsons referred to one of the remedies Cyrus suggested to Croesus, king of Lydia, for dealing with the revolt of the Lydians, namely to make them wear tunics.[4] She described it as

a discipline which proved as effective in changing their manners as that of Nurse when she makes her naughty little charge put on his sister's dress or hat. Is not part of the severity of his punishment due to the dread in the boy's mind that he will not merely look like but become a girl?[5]

She mentions 'Nurse's' punishment as a matter of common occurrence and is one of the first writers to recognise its existence. Her comment on its effects is perceptive but she does not seem to disapprove of it. Some years earlier an actual 'Nurse', did not go quite as far as this. She found it was sufficient merely to change the name of the boy without changing his clothes. In the first of the memoirs I am going to quote, Eleanor Acland, born in 1878, records the cruel behaviour of Nurse Barley. Her brother George was born in 1879 and this is a punishment suffered by him alone.

There was one other punishment, meted out to George. He was a submissive, aloof little person, who would put up with a good deal more nagging and snubbing than Milly [Eleanor Acland]. But once his gentleness snapped, it snapped altogether, and he would kick out at Barley's shins with all his might and main.
'Very well, Master George,' Barley would say. 'You'll wear your card when we go for our walk.'
Upon which George would beseech her. 'No, no, Barley, not my card. Oh, I'm sorry. I will be good. Please not my card.'
But Barley with her sore shins would not be in a relenting mood, so when we set forth on our nursery walk there would be tied round George's neck a card bearing the inscription:
GEORGINA SHE KICKS[6]

Nurse Barley thus employed a David Copperfield type of notice combined with a change of sex. While George still wore petticoats of course a label of this sort would sufficiently designate him as female. Miss Paraman made Curzon wear a petticoat because he had been breeched already.

The next example is one that a friend came across entirely by chance while we were looking at books on the second-hand shelves of a bookshop. She picked up the autobiography of the French cabaret star, Mistinguett, and found this.

> My father died when I was still very young–he scratched his hand on some chicken wire and his arm swelled. I think he must have had tetanus. My mother carried on alone, running the business and bringing myself and my two brothers up. The younger of the two, Marcel, was my favourite. I used to look after him, take him to school, and boss him like any elder sister. When he was naughty, I punished him by dressing him up as a girl. Even now, as a grown man, he reproaches me gently from time to time for putting him in petticoats all those years ago.[7]

Mistinguett does not give her age, but she must have been born about 1880, so the naughty Marcel was probably obliged to put on girl's clothes in the eighteen nineties, again suggesting that this was a period when the application of the punishment became more widespread. Confirmation of this is provided by a correspondent to the popular weekly *Reveille* who gave his name and address. A reader had complained on 30 December 1949 that his mother, mother-in-law and wife were proposing to put his sons aged eleven and thirteen into corsets to cure their stooping. Two readers wrote in favour of corsets.

> For instance, there's F.L. Robinson of Wood Street, Birkenhead, who says that when he was a lad, fifty years ago, a favourite way of punishing boys was to dress them in female garments. 'I have spent evening after evening dressed in a complete set of my sisters' clothes,' he writes, 'bodice, stays (and they *were* stays in those days), frilled petticoats, a short frock, long stockings, and high button boots.'
> Despite that Mr Robinson thinks corsets will cure stooping.
> Then there's James Goodman of Fulham Palace-road, London S.W. 'When I was fifteen and my two brothers were thirteen and twelve, we were all tightly laced up in corsets by mother to stop us raiding orchards. They certainly checked our boisterous ways, and we have carried on wearing them to this day.'[8]

I have already quoted some passages from the children's story, *Goin' On Fourteen*. I am very grateful to a friend for drawing my attention to what is perhaps the earliest reference in fiction to the punishment of a boy by making him wear his sister's clothes, namely in Barrie's *The Little White Bird* published in 1902. James Matthew Barrie married the actress Mary Ansell on 9 July 1894 and they moved into their first house, 133, Gloucester Road in March 1895. Walking in the nearby Kensington Gardens, Barrie met the Llewelyn Davies boys, George and Jack, then aged five and four, in 1898. Over the next few years Barrie became friends with the whole family and as he played with the boys in the Gardens and at his country home, ideas for the novel mentioned and the play, *Peter Pan* gradually developed. *The Little White Bird* is a fictional account of the relationship between Barrie and George, with Barrie disguised as the narrator, Captain W....., and George as 'David'.[9] The chapter entitled 'Grand Tour of the Gardens' contains this passage.

> We are now in the Broad Walk, and it is as much bigger than the other walks as your father is bigger than you. . . . In the Broad Walk you meet all the people who are worth knowing, and there is usually a grown-up with them to prevent their going on the

Costume pour jeune garçon
de 8 à 9 ans.
(Patron découpé.)
N° 327.

Costumes d'enfants.
Robe en toile pour petite fille
de 7 à 8 ans.

Robe pour petite fille
de 9 à 10 ans.
(Patron découpé.)
N° 328.

Modèles des *Magasins du Louvre*.

23.   Costumes for Children Seven to Ten.   *La Mode Illustrée*, 25 June 1899, p.308.

damp grass, and to make them stand disgraced at the corner of a seat if they have been mad-dog or Mary-Annish. To be Mary-Annish is to behave like a girl, whimpering because nurse won't carry you, or simpering with your thumb in your mouth, and it is a hateful quality; but to be mad-dog is to kick out at everything, and there is some satisfaction in that.

If I were to point out all the notable places as we pass up the Broad Walk, it would be time to turn back before we reach them, and I simply wave my stick at Cecco Hewlett's Tree, that memorable spot where a boy called Cecco lost his penny, and, looking for it, found twopence. There has been a good deal of excavation going on there ever since. Farther up the walk is the little wooden house in which Marmaduke Perry hid. There is no more awful story of the Gardens than this of Marmaduke Perry, who had been Mary-Annish three days in succession, and was sentenced to appear in the Broad Walk dressed in his sister's clothes. He hid in the little wooden house, and refused to emerge until they brought him knickerbockers with pockets.[10]

Cecco Hewlett was the real son of the writer and Barrie's friend, Maurice Hewlett, so the discovery of the pennies may well have happened. 'Mad-dogs' remind us of George Acland kicking Nurse Barley, but in Kensington Gardens it is apparently the 'Mary-Anns' who are dressed as girls. That is to say, the punishment fits the crime. Boys must be boys. If you behave like a girl, you are made to appear in public dressed as one. No one seems to have identified a real Marmaduke Perry and his hiding in the wooden house is probably fiction, but it is quite possible that Barrie heard of an actual instance of this punishment from his young friends in the Gardens. The concept of the 'Mary-Ann' does seem more appropriate to the nannies of Kensington Gardens than to Barrie's Scottish background.

Another popular writer whose name was referred to me in this connection by someone who didn't wish to be acknowledged, although I do thank her very sincerely, is Lucy Maud Montgomery (1874-1942). Born in Prince Edward Island of Scottish descent, Montgomery taught for three years before marrying Ewan MacDonald, a Presbyterian minister, in 1911. Meanwhile in 1908 she had already published her first novel, *Anne of Green Gables*, which was set in Prince Edward Island at the turn of the century. The six-year-old twins, Davy and Dora, are adopted by Marilla in chapter 8 of the second book, *Anne of Avonlea* (1911). In the fourth book, *Anne of the Island* (1915), Anne, now eighteen, has gone to Redmond College in 'Kingsport'. She receives letters from home. One, from Mrs Lynde, reports a punishment suffered by Davy, now eight.

> Davy has been pretty good since you went away. One day he was bad and Marilla punished him by making him wear Dora's apron all day, and then he went out and cut all Dora's aprons up. I spanked him for that and then he went and chased my rooster to death. (p. 43)

Rainbow Valley (c. 1919) does not belong to the Avonlea series, although Marilla is mentioned as now being eighty-five years of age. It concerns the new minister at 'Glen St. Mary', a widower named Meredith with four young children. The children, Gerald twelve, Faith eleven, Una ten and Thomas Carlyle (Carl) nine, are looked after by Aunt Martha aged seventy-five. One evening the children sing hymns in the graveyard having forgotten that the Methodists are holding a prayer meeting at the same time. A few days later, Mr Meredith, having learnt of this, calls them into his study.

> They went in, somewhat awed. It was such an unusual thing for their father to do. What could he be going to say to them? They racked their memories for any recent transgression of sufficient importance, but could not recall any. Carl had spilled a sauc-

erful of jam on Mrs Peter Flagg's silk dress two evenings before, when, at Aunt Martha's invitation, she had stayed to supper. But Mr Meredith had not noticed it, and Mrs Flagg, who was a kindly soul, had made no fuss. Besides, Carl had been punished by having to wear Una's dress all the rest of the evening. (pp. 283-4)

The theory seems to be that having damaged a female garment Carl has to wear one himself as a penance. He wears the dress of the sister nearest to himself in age. All these fictional examples, and there may be more to discover, are inserted into the narrative quite incidentally. They are not necessary to the plot and I suggest that they have come into the authors' minds through recollection of real incidents or stories they have heard. I see them therefore as useful evidence of the sort of thing that went on during the dozen or so years on either side of 1900.

1   Havelock Ellis, *Studies in the Psychology of Sex*, 7 vols (Philadelphia: F.A. Davis Company, 1928), VII ('Eonism and other Supplementary Studies') 56-63.
2   George W. Henry, *Sex Variants* (New York: Paul B. Hoeber, 1948, first published 1941) p. 505.
3   Louis S. London, *Abnormal Sexual Behaviour* (New York: Julian Press, 1937) p. 167.
4   Herodotus, *Histories*, I, 155.
5   Elsie Clews Parsons, *The Old Fashioned Woman* (New York: G.P. Putnam's Sons, 1913), p. 170.
6   Eleanor Acland, *Goodbye for the Present. The Story of Two Childhoods, Milly 1878-88 & Ellen 1913-24* (London: Hodder and Stoughton, 1935), p. 32 (cited by Jonathan Gathorne-Hardy, *The Rise and Fall of the British Nanny* (London: Hodder and Stoughton, 1972), pp. 278-80).
7   Mistinguett, *Mistinguett, Queen of the Paris Night*, trans. Lucienne Hill (London: Elek Books, 1954), p. 2.
8   *Reveille*, 13 January 1950, p. 4.
9   Andrew Birkin, *J.M. Barrie & The Lost Boys* (London: Constable & Co., 1979).
10   J.M. Barrie, *The Little White Bird* (London: Hodder and Stoughton, 1902), pp. 129-30.